Photo Crafts sourcebook

Thunder Bay Press
An imprint of the Advantage Publishers Group
5880 Oberlin Drive, San Diego, CA 92121-4794
www.thunderbaybooks.com

All notations of errors or omissions should be addressed to Thunder Bay Press, Editorial Department, at
the above address. All other correspondence (author inquiries, permissions) concerning the content of this
book should be addressed to Rockport Publishers, Inc., 33 Commercial Street, Gloucester, MA 01930-5089.
Telephone: (978) 283-9590; Fax: (978) 283-2742; www.rockpub.com.

ISBN: 1-59223-217-5

Library of Congress Cataloging-in-Publication data available upon request.

Grateful acknowledgment is given to Livia McRee for her from work from *Easy Transfers for Any Surface*
on pages 10–35, 40–79, 82–101, 250–251, and 280–297; to Mary Ann Hall for her work from *Crafter's
Project Book* on pages 36–39, 216–217, and 262–269; to Barbara Matthiessen for her work from *New
Metal Foil Crafts* on pages 80–81 and 274–279; to Laurie Klein for her work from *Handcoloring for Black
and White Photography* on pages 104–215; to Jason Thompson for his work from *Making Journals by
Hand* on pages 218–219 and 222–229; to Jessica Wrobel for her work from *Crafter's Recipe Book* on pages
220–221; to Lisa Kerr for her work from *Paper Card Book* on pages 230–245 and 270–273; to Kathy Cano
Murillo for her work from *Making Shadow Boxes and Shrines* on pages 248–249; to Lynne Farris for her
work from *Baby Crafts* on pages 252–255; and to Barbara Mauriello for her work from *Making Memeory
Books* on pages 256–261.

1 2 3 4 5 08 07 06 05 04

Printed in China

Photo Crafts Sourcebook

Projects and Ideas for Making Photos Fun

Laurie Klein and Livia McRee

THUNDER BAY
P·R·E·S·S

San Diego, California

Contents

Introduction

Taking pictures has never been easier or more fun. Advances in technology have made it possible to take, develop, and print pictures at home, as well as crop, manipulate, merge, and send them wherever we want electronically.

Scrapbooking and memory making have become household words and continue to be two of the largest and fasting growing areas of the craft industry. People have always craved the ability to record a moment visually or commemorate a special event in a special way.

As a result of this growth in photo manipulation and scrapbooking and although people have always used photos to display memories, there has never before been such an outpouring of creative ways to use photographs in decorative and commemorative crafts.

Photo Crafts Sourcebook is the first book to address photos as the inspiration for crafts. Packed with step-by-step projects and featuring everything from the fine art of hand-coloring your black-and-white pictures to scrapbook projects that use the newest and most exciting materials to making your own frames and photo albums, this is *the* idea and instruction resource for photo crafts.

Flipping through these pages, you will find a broad range of craft mediums that incorporate photography. Techniques for photo transfers to fabric, wood, and ceramics, instructions for hand-coloring photography, as well as ideas for gifts, journals, cards, and home accessories are all included.

Old photos or new ones, this book has something for anyone who is looking for creative ways to use that shoebox full of photographic moments in time.

Photo Transfers

Finding *Artwork*

Seek out artwork for crafting with transfers the same way a graphic designer would hunt down an image for a professional assignment. A trip to the art-technique section of a bookstore, a visit to an online stock image archive, or a spin through a CD-ROM image collection can result in some great finds.

CLIP ART

Clip art is a generic term for copyright-free images, such as illustrations, borders, and backgrounds, that were created for commercial or decorative purposes and are now compiled into books or on CD-ROMs, available for use in new works. The style and variety of available clip art is staggering—from 1930s illustrated advertisements to cigar box labels, Indian textile prints to Celtic illuminated borders. This "recycled" artwork is a staple for graphic artists and transfer artists alike.

Large bookstores usually have sections dedicated to the subject of art technique. It is usually in this section that clip art books can be found. Many books are packaged with a CD-ROM, which contains professional scans of all of the book's artwork. This is not only timesaving, but also enables anyone with a printer and computer—but no scanner—to work digitally. See Resources on page 298 for information on clip art publishers.

ONLINE STOCK IMAGE PROVIDERS

Browse thousands of images by keyword with online stock image providers. Enter a keyword or two, click a button, and all the corresponding images in the database will pop up on a virtual light board. A digital watermark on the images indicates copyright protection. Many online stock image providers only cater to the professional market and charge hundreds of dollars for one image. However, for a few dollars, a company called Corbis (www.corbis.com) will allow images to be downloaded for non-commercial use. In other words, use them freely to make gifts and home decorating projects, but don't open up a store to sell the crafts.

MAKING IMAGES

Personal and family photos, children's drawings, pressed leaves and flowers, scraps of old paper, fabric, and just about any other fairly flat material can be used to make images for use in transfer projects. Start thinking of new ways to combine such materials to create collages for projects. Ticket stubs or interesting receipts from a memorable trip layered around a photo can creatively capture the essence of time spent with friends or family. Transfer this image to a canvas or a box top for a truly special, personal craft.

WHAT'S FREE TO USE?

Since copiers and scanners make it so easy and appealing to duplicate images, copyright concerns have become increasingly prevalent. For the craftsperson and artist, it's often tricky to determine what can be duplicated freely and what restrictions, if any, apply to that use. Here are a few things to take note:

- Some, but not all, copyrighted works are marked with the copyright symbol—©. Keep in mind that photographs are copyrighted by the photographer unless otherwise specified in writing. All published materials, including images from magazines and books, are also copyrighted.

- It is a common misconception that scanning a copyrighted image and then slightly changing it using image-editing software is a way to circumvent copyright restrictions, but this is not the case. In fact, it is viewed as destroying the integrity and value of the original work and can result in additional penalties. It is perfectly acceptable, though, to use an image as reference to create an original work.

- Copyrights do expire, and published materials more than fifty years old fall into the public domain unless the copyright is renewed. The drawing on a store receipt that has been out of business for one hundred years is most likely safe to use, but a photo in an old book that's been recently reprinted is not.

- Many copyrighted images can be used with permission. Call or write to the company or publisher that owns the image and describe how the image will be used. To be safe, be sure to get permission in writing. Send a self-addressed, stamped postcard with a sentence or two that grants permission for the use of a specific image. Then all the recipient needs to do is sign and return the card.

- While copyright laws and restrictions can be disheartening, remember that they are in place to protect the creators of images—including you. To officially copyright an original image of your own, simply place your name, the © symbol, and the year on the work. Then write to the Copyright Office, Library of Congress, Washington, D.C. 20559, requesting a form to register the copyright for a small fee.

- When in doubt, play it safe. There are plenty of copyright-free sources for images—starting in the Gallery of Art for Projects section of this book.

Modifying Art *by* Hand and Computer

The artwork for transfers can be prepared by hand using traditional methods or by computer using image-editing software. Both ways will yield gorgeous results. The most important thing to remember is that the quality of the final image will be no better than the original—whether working by hand or on a computer. And, since virtually anything flat can be scanned or copied, there's no limit to the kinds of images that can become a transfer.

BY HAND

When preparing artwork by hand, it is usually necessary to have several copies of the same image. For example, to make the table runner on page 32, first make color copies of the butterfly artwork several times and in several sizes. Then, cut each butterfly out and mount them on a piece of white cardstock using spray adhesive. This way, only one piece of precious transfer paper is necessary for the project. The rigidity of cardstock will help prevent the images from wrinkling or peeling off by accident, and the spray adhesive provides a smooth, even bond that will minimize the shadows that can appear when copying a piece of layered paper. Since color copies can get expensive, do all design work using a black-and-white copier. Determine all copying percentages before using a color copier.

Try modifying artwork directly by using colored pencils and paint, or splice together patterns to create borders. Heat transfer sheets can also be drawn on before the image is ironed in place; just be sure not to scratch through to the paper beneath—unless that's the desired effect.

USING COLOR COPIERS

Color copies can be used to do many of the same things that image-editing software does, including drastic or minimal color adjustments and image reversals. The best way to learn what a color copier can do is to experiment with one at a shop that sets aside a few machines for self-service.

Since color copying machines are extremely expensive—and using ink jet transfer paper in a color copier will cause major damage—be sure to bring heat transfer paper in its original packaging to the shop. That way, the clerk can be sure that the paper will not ruin the copier. It's also a good idea to ask the local copy shop what kind of copier it has, then purchase papers that specify compatibility with that type of machine. Some copy shops also supply transfer paper.

BY COMPUTER

In order to create and print out transfers by computer, a scanner and image-editing software will be necessary. First and foremost, read the manuals for both thoroughly and follow the recommendations made for specific types of images or effects, such as black-and-white images, printer resolutions, and so on.

SCANNING IMAGES

A decent, easy-to-use flatbed scanner can be purchased for seventy-five to one hundred dollars. It is a fantastic, inspiring tool that transforms an ordinary computer into a remarkable crafting tool. Since color copies can be one to two dollars each, a scanner is a cost-effective investment for the transfer artist.

Basically, scanners need to be told what is being scanned and how to scan it. Is it a photo or a magazine print? What size should it be? Is it in color or black and white? Don't worry. The scanner's software will create an interface that will ask all these questions, so it is simply a matter of checking the right box.

The resolution of the image is another important scanning element that needs to be selected. Resolution is referred to as dpi, or dots per inch. These dots translate into color when the image is printed, and the more dots there are, the sharper and more detailed the image. *For the projects in this book, 150 dpi is sufficient; files with high resolutions take up a lot of memory on a computer and will slow it down.*

IMAGE EDITING

Some scanners are sold with very basic image-editing software, which is great for being introduced to the whole process. But for less than one hundred dollars much more sophisticated programs, such as Adobe Photoshop Elements, provide an intriguing tool. Based on the original Adobe Photoshop, which is an expensive and complex program used by professionals, Elements provides a startling array of possibilities for modifying artwork with an intuitive and fun-to-use interface. For example, a scanned photo can be turned into a watercolor image with literally the touch of a button.

Tip:

When working with a digital file, save it frequently under different names throughout the design process. Then, it will be easy to go back to a certain point and start from there. It also encourages experimentation, since there is no need to worry about ruining the one and only version of an image. As with any work on a computer, it's always a good idea to save often.

The best thing about image editing on a computer is speed. Lighten a dark photo, erase unwanted areas, add a background color—all these changes can be made quite easily and quickly. It's also a snap to change the size or color of an image, make several copies of it, and rotate it in any direction.

PRINTING

Good color printers can also be purchased for less than one hundred dollars. The ink, however, is fairly expensive; so when printing out test sheets, select the economy mode, which uses less ink. Always run a test on a piece of paper before printing on a transfer sheet. There are often details that need to be adjusted, even when everything looks fine on the computer screen. For example, a horizontal document needs to be printed on landscape mode or the image will get cropped. This is something that's very easy to forget, and there are no visual clues until the document is printed. Finally, it's best to load transfer sheets one at a time, and print them one by one. Since they are different in thickness and consistency than standard paper, they can jam printers if several pages are loaded at once.

Transfers *to Fabric*

Fabric is the traditional surface for transfers, so photos and artwork can be integrated into just about any sewing project, from table runners to pillows. The possibilities are seemingly endless. With so many methods and products now available specially formulated for fabric, it's easy to create distinctive transfers that suit a project perfectly. As for those who don't sew, don't be intimidated. There are many ways to craft with fabric without sewing a stitch. ❧ Experiment with the techniques described in this book to discover the qualities of each. Transfers can be glossy or matte, transparent or opaque, stiff or flexible, and each finish coveys a different mood and style. Combine different types of fabrics with various transfer techniques—not only to determine what works best, but also to make new and interesting discoveries. And always use an appropriate iron setting for the fabric, even if the transfer method suggests a higher heat setting. ❧ When working with fabric, remember that the smoother and finer it is, the more completely the image will transfer. Coarser material, such as linen, can also be used but the image may transfer incompletely, resulting in an aged, antique look. This additional element of texture can be appealing as well as useful for many kinds of projects too. Generally, cotton, polyester, and cotton/polyester blends are the easiest fabrics to work with, but experimentation will certainly lead to great discoveries. Finally, before using fabric, always wash and dry by machine and press, especially if the fabric will get wet or washed in the future.

Techniques and Tips
for Fabric Transfers

There are a variety of products specifically designed for fabric transfers, making it easy to achieve just about any look imaginable. Each method, of course, has its own advantages and disadvantages, so consider what quality is most important for the finished product. Some of these qualities include durability, matching the original image as closely as possible, translucency, and softness.

TRANSFER METHODS

HEAT TRANSFER PAPER

The easiest, fastest way to transfer images to fabric is with heat transfer paper. It takes three basic steps: print or copy the image onto the paper, cut away the excess, and iron it in place. There are many brands of heat transfer paper available, most of which offer translucent heat transfer paper, so the color of the fabric merges with the transfer. In all the white areas of the design, it will be the color and texture of the fabric that dominates. For this reason, white or light fabric colors often work best. Solid, dark-colored artwork, however, can be successfully transferred to dark fabrics. Also available are opaque heat transfer sheets, which can be transferred to any color fabric. All white areas of the design will remain pure white. The process is a little different from standard heat transferring, in that the transfer is peeled off of a backing sheet first. Once the transfer is positioned on fabric, a silicon pressing sheet, which is included with the paper, is used to safely iron the transfer in place.

Tips & Tricks for Heat Transfer Sheets

- The transfer will be a mirror image of the original—so don't forget to reverse the artwork when transferring or it will read backwards. Copiers have a setting for this, as do image-editing programs. This step isn't necessary, however, with opaque heat transfer paper.

- Use firm pressure and a circular motion to iron transfers in place. It should take only thirty seconds to a couple of minutes to adhere a transfer to fabric. (The finer the fabric the quicker the transfer.) Once the transfer has heated up, use lighter pressure with the iron because the transfer will be malleable and prone to smearing at this point.

- The manufacturer of a particular brand of transfer paper will usually have suggested settings for the iron temperature. Some, however, do not. Generally, use an appropriate setting for the type of fabric being used. If the transfer becomes cracked or crazed try a lower setting and iron for a shorter period of time. If the transfer doesn't seem to be taking very well, try a higher setting and iron for a longer period of time.

- Peeling a transfer when still warm yields a matte finish, while peeling a transfer when cool yields a shinier finish.

- Check if a transfer is complete by peeling up one corner. If it is still sticking to the backing paper in spots, simply iron the area again.

- Pay special attention to the edges of the transfer to be sure they are completely fused. These areas are often the most difficult.

- If an area of the transfer bubbles up or starts to peel after the backing is removed, just cover that area with a piece of the used backing (one that doesn't have any residual bits of transfer left on it) and go over the area again.

- Also note that fabric with transferred images, including printable fabric, is more resistant to pins and needles. Take this into consideration when sewing, and use a machine whenever possible.

PRINTABLE FABRIC

This specially coated, backed fabric can be used with ink jet printers and copiers. Both washable and nonwashable kinds are available, so be sure to check the package before purchasing. June Tailor's washable, colorfast Printer Fabric is a good choice, because it yields dependable results. The sheets are available in white and off-white. Printable fabric is fairly expensive, so always print on paper first to check for any problems with artwork. Then print on the fabric when the design is finalized.

Tips & Tricks for Printable Fabric

- Before printing, check for any bumps on the surface of the fabric and carefully pick them off. Often, these will come off after rinsing the fabric, and will result in a white spot if they aren't pulled off beforehand.

- Follow the manufacturer's directions for rinsing fabric to make it colorfast. Have dry, absorbent towels on hand as well. Press the rinsed fabric between the towels to squeeze out all excess water, then lay flat to dry. This helps prevent colors from bleeding, which can be especially undesirable if there is type in the design.

- Printable fabric will shrink anywhere from $1/8$" (3 mm) to $1/2$" (1 cm) after rinsing, so it's crucial to measure the fabric as you cut it, rather than depending on the image for sizing.

- Add a matching, colored border around the artwork for the seam allowance. It will also compensate for shrinkage and prevent any white from peeking through when piecing a project together.

LIQUID TRANSFER MEDIUM

This medium, which is available in clear and opaque formulas, creates a permanent and washable transfer. Simply brush the liquid on a photocopy, then place the paper face down on a piece of fabric and gently smooth it out with a sponge brush or by rolling the bottle of medium over it. Try not to apply too much pressure or the medium will ooze out from under the paper. The transfer then has to dry twenty-four to forty-eight hours, depending on humidity. Once dry, remove the paper backing by saturating it with a damp sponge, then rubbing it off.

Tips & Tricks for Liquid Transfer Medium

- An old credit card makes a great tool for applying the medium smoothly and evenly, with a minimum of effort.

- Leave a small tab or two of extra paper on the transfer when trimming it out to making handling and placing it on the fabric easier.

- Although liquid transfer medium works best with photocopies, ink jet printouts on photo-quality, matte-finish paper can also be used. Printouts tend to wrinkle when they absorb the medium, and these wrinkles cause the medium to dry in unattractive ridges. Try printout transfers no larger than 3" (8 cm) or 4" (10 cm) and with a thin coat of transfer medium, then place them immediately on the fabric to minimize this effect.

- When using liquid transfer medium, there is no need to worry about crazing or peeling, which can sometimes be a problem with heat transfers.

- Take into consideration that these kinds of transfers should not be ironed or dry-cleaned when planning a project.

Memory *Art Canvas*

A prestretched canvas is the perfect choice for creating a commemorative photographic compilation like this one, which chronicles the fun, romantic weekend one couple had in Venice Beach, California. So dig up all those vacation, party, or holiday photos and start photocopying or scanning them to make the perfect gift for friends and family. Liquid transfer medium is the best choice for stretched canvas, which is awkward to iron evenly. Also, color copies work best with this method. (Be sure to read *Tips & Tricks for Liquid Transfer Medium* on page 19 for more information.) To finish the project, try painting the edges of the canvas for a quick faux-frame.

MATERIALS

- *prestretched canvas*

- *clear liquid transfer medium*

- *craft knife or scissors*

- *sponge brush applicator*

- *large sponge*

Starting *Out*

Tinting photos in various, fun shades is easy to do with any image-editing program. Consult the application's guidebook for specific methods, or have a photocopy clerk adjust the hues.

STEP 1

Prepare the transfers. Photocopy or scan and print out the photographs to be used. Play with the size and arrangement of the photos, and lighten or darken the images if necessary. The colors of the images can be manipulated with a copier or a computer (see page 12, *Modifying Art by Hand and Computer*). Next, get a color copy of the prepared artwork. If using an inkjet printer, use a high-quality matte-finish paper and the paper's corresponding setting for the printer. Then have a color copy made of the print out. Don't forget to flip the image, if desired. Let the paper dry for thirty minutes before proceeding.

STEP 2

Brush the medium on the canvas and adhere the transfer. Cut the transfer out along the edge of the image with scissors or a craft knife. The canvas used here is 8" x 10" (20 cm x 25 cm), so only one piece of paper was needed. For a larger canvas, tape together the pieces of paper on the reverse side. Be sure to align the seams carefully. Brush a thick, even coat of transfer medium on the canvas using a sponge brush applicator. The coat should be about $1/16$" (1.5 mm) thick. Next, lay the artwork face down on the medium. Use a bottle or a brayer to gently smooth the transfer and press it into the medium. Let the transfer dry for twenty-four to forty-eight hours, depending on humidity.

STEP 3

<u>Remove the paper transfer with a sponge</u>. Moisten the entire transfer
with a damp sponge and wait a few minutes for the water to saturate
the paper. Then, use the sponge to rub the paper off the canvas
using a circular motion. Let the surface dry. If there are any clouded
areas, which indicate residual paper, rub the surface again with a
damp sponge.

Variation:

Experiment with image-
editing "filters" to modify a
single photo. The watercolor
filter in Adobe Photoshop
Elements was used here for
a painted look. For more
tips on modifying art by
computer, see page 13.

Commemorative *Collage Pillow*

The frame for this photo of my grandfather was made using various ID cards, which tell some of his life story and commemorate his many roles. Ordinary, old documents often have interesting graphic elements, and they confer history and lineage to a project. Approach the design of the pillow as a biographical journey to create an interesting, effective, and highly personal collage. Try using diplomas, birth certificates, passports, awards, or newspaper clippings of special events. Then, focus on the most important parts of each, like names, signatures, or seals, making sure they are highly visible in the collage. Before assembling the collage, adjust the value of the images so that they are similar by using a using a photocopier or a computer. This will create a unified design with a patterned effect.

MATERIALS

- *1 sheet of printer fabric*

- *½ yard (46 cm) of fabric for border and back of pillow*

- *14" x 14" (36 cm x 36 cm) pillow form*

- *straight pins*

- *needle and thread*

- *scissors or rotary cutter*

- *cutting mat*

- *clear ruler*

- *optional: sewing machine*

Starting *Out*

Before beginning the project, be sure to wash the fabric for the border and the back of the pillow to remove any residual chemicals from the manufacturing process.

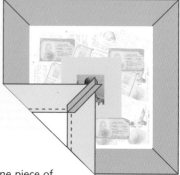

STEP 1

Prepare and print out artwork. Photocopy or scan and print out the photographs and items to be used for the collage. Play with the size and arrangement of the images (see page 12, *Modifying Art by Hand and Computer*). Make the final piece of art 8" (20 cm) square, then print it onto or have it copied to the fabric sheet. Trim the fabric so that there is a 1/4" (5 mm) white border around the image.

STEP 2

Assemble the pillowcase. Cut one piece of 14 1/2" x 14 1/2" (37 cm x 37 cm) fabric for the pillow back and four pieces of 3 1/2" x 14 1/2" (9 cm x 37 cm) fabric for the border. Next, center the border strips along each edge of the printer fabric and pin in place. The pieces will overlap at each corner. Stitch each border strip in place, starting and stopping 1/4" (5 mm) from the corners of the printer fabric. Press the seam allowances towards the printer fabric. Then, miter each corner. To do this, bring the outer edges of both border strips together, pin them in place, and mark a 45 degree angle extending from the corner of the printer fabric to the outer edge of the border strips. Sew along this line, then trim 1/4" (5 mm) from the seam. Press the seam allowances open.

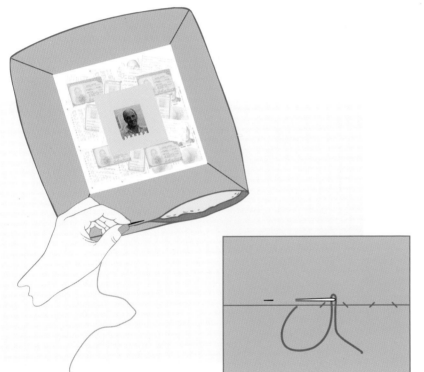

STEP 3

Stuff and close the pillow. Pin the pillow back to the pillow front,
right sides together. Stitch $1/4$" (5 mm) from the edges of the pillow,
leaving an 8" (20 cm) opening at the bottom of the pillow for turn-
ing. Then, clip the corners diagonally to reduce bulk. Next, turn the
pillow cover right side out and insert the pillow form. Finally, slipstitch
the opening closed.

Variation:

Silky satin paired with a central pattern like this illustrated Chinese illustrated lotus, makes an elegant, easy
pillow. Most iron-on transfer sheets
will work well with 100 percent polyester fabric, such as satin; check the
package for specific recommendations. Choose a light or white color
that won't obscure the transfer, and
be sure to hold the slippery fabric
taut and in place while ironing. Then,
assemble the pillow as described for
the main project, but use two pieces
of fabric cut to the same size. The art for
this project can be found on page 282.

Indian *Folk Art Bag*

The soft, natural colors of canvas and wood are perfect complements to the colorful, nature-inspired themes of the hand-painted Indian folk art used on this bag. A simple iron-on transfer is the best and easiest method for the smooth surface of canvas. Use transparent heat transfer paper so that the color and texture of the canvas blends with the artwork, enhancing the hand-painted feel. Try using a coarser, more open fabric such as jute or burlap for a rustic look. Also, remember to launder and machine-dry the bag before decorating. Any shrinkage in the fabric will damage the transfer.

MATERIALS

- *plain canvas tote bag*
- *heat transfer paper*
- *metallic fabric paint*
- *craft knife or scissors*
- *thin paint brush*
- *iron*

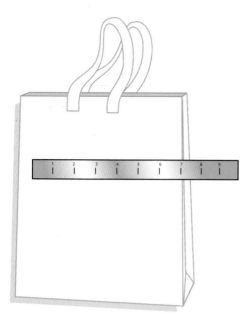

Starting *Out*

Try adding a simple, painted border around the transfer to accentuate the folk art motif. A linear border followed by a dotted border was used here for a traditional Indian textile look. The art for these projects can be found on page 282.

STEP 1

Prepare the transfer and the bag. Measure the tote bag to determine the how large the artwork needs to be. Then, photocopy or print the artwork onto a heat transfer sheet, following the manufacturer's instructions. Press out any creases in the tote bag and snip off any imperfections, such as nubs of fabric that may interfere with the transfer.

STEP 2

Cut out the transfer. Use scissors or a craft knife, a cutting mat, and a ruler. Cut as closely to the artwork as possible, without cutting into it.

STEP 3

Iron the transfer in place. Again, follow the manufacturer's directions. A medium heat setting works best for transferring onto fabric. Tack the center of the transfer down first, then the edges. It will take thirty seconds to a minute to complete the transfer. Let the transfer cool for several seconds before checking to see if it has been completely transferred. If it resists peeling, then let it cool completely. Add a metallic hand-painted border if desired.

Variation:

Vintage luggage labels from the golden age of travel—that is, when people traveled by sea instead of by air—are works of art in their own right. Scatter a bunch on a tote bag for an instant world-traveler look. Use the same method described for the folk art bag to transfer the labels.

Indonesian *Table Runner*

Try using printer fabric to replicate beautiful patterns from antique fabric. Many clip-art books contain full-color photographs of actual fabrics, including details such as embroidered embellishments. Using these gorgeous, handmade designs will lend an air of sophistication and history to a project. The batik design used here makes a sumptuous runner when bordered with shiny, elegant black and silver fabric. Repeat the image as necessary to create a runner to fit any table. Then, add a simple border in a contrasting color to make the design pop out.

MATERIALS

- *printable fabric*

- *½ yard (46 cm) of black satin*

- *¼ yard (23 cm) of silver satin*

- *invisible nylon thread*

- *scissors or rotary cutter*

- *cutting mat*

- *clear ruler*

- *straight pins*

- *needle*

- *optional: sewing machine*

Starting *Out*

Determine how large the runner needs to be by beginning with the size of artwork cut from the printer fabric. Then, sketch out the design on a piece of graph paper to keep track of how many pieces of fabric are necessary to make the runner. The art for these projects can be found on pages 284 and 285.

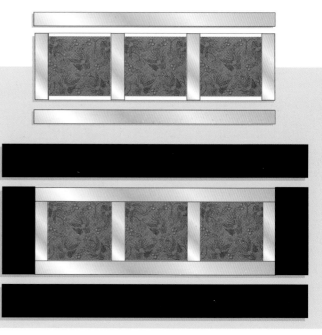

STEP 1

Prepare and print out artwork. Scan the art, making sure it is 8" (20 cm) square, then print it out on the fabric sheet following the manufacturer's instructions. Print as many sheets as needed for the runner. Be sure to read Tips & Tricks for Printable Fabric on page 19. Then, trim the fabric leaving a 1/4" (5 mm) white border around the image.

STEP 2

Make the runner top. Machine-wash and dry the satin, then press To make the 1" (3 cm) silver border, first cut 1 1/2" by 8 1/2" (4 c x 22 cm) strips to separate each printer fabric panel. For the featur runner, which has three printer fabric panels, four separating strips are needed. Sew the panels together with a silver strip in between each, and on both ends. Press the seams open to flatten the piecec panels. To complete the top and bottom of the silver border, cut tv strips measuring 1 1/2" (4 cm) wide by the length of pieced panel, and adding 1/2" (1 cm) for the seam allowance. Sew the strips into place. To make the outer black border, cut two 3 1/2" by 8 1/2" (9 cm x 22 cm) strips and sew them to each short end of the piece panel. This will create a 3" (8 cm) wide black border when the run ner is complete. To complete the top and bottom of the black bord cut two strips measuring 3 1/2" (9 cm) wide by the length of pieced pan adding 1/2" (1 cm) for the seam allowance. Sew the strips into plac

STEP 3

Stitch the runner top and back together. Measure the pieced runner top, and cut a piece of fabric for the back that is exactly the same size. Pin the runner top and back together about 1" (3 cm) from the edges, fronts facing. Then, stitch 1/4" (5 mm) in from the edges, using a sewing machine or a needle and thread. Leave an opening along one short end large enough to turn the runner right side out. Clip the corners diagonally to reduce bulk, then turn the runner right side out. Slipstitch the opening closed (see page 27).

Variation:

This easy-to-sew table runner can be made in an afternoon. It makes a light, airy accent to bring a bit of summer to any room. Plain, store-bought or antique linens are also perfect candidates for decorating with a few quick transfers. The butterflies here were made using pressed larkspur and rose petals. Try using other flowers or plants to personalize artwork for transferring. The variety of floral shapes and colors is sure to inspire creativity. First, press petals in a phone book until they are dry. Then arrange them on a piece of white paper using tiny dabs of glue to secure them. Then, photocopy or scan them to make transfers.

ARTIST: MARGARET TIBERIO

A simple lampshade is transformed by transferring images from slide photographs to fabric using the Polaroid image transfer process. The special print film has an extended tonal range that enhances the dreamy, watercolor-like hues of the original photographs, making the final transfers glow in the lamplight. This sophisticated decorating technique is appropriate for any series of images, from landscape panoramas to architectural details. Imperfections in the transferred prints add interest to the final piece.

photo-transfer
lampshade

Makes one lampshade

1 Expose your chosen slide in the slide printer onto the appropriate Polaroid instant print film specified by printer manufacturer. The film and printer types determine the size of the print. See package information for more details.

2 Rough-cut a piece of fabric large enough to hold selected print size. Soak in warm water and place damp fabric onto a glass pane or other smooth, hard surface. Excess water should be blotted from the fabric.

3 Pull the exposed film through the rollers of the slide printer. Wait ten seconds, then peel the image apart. Quickly place the negative carefully onto the fabric. With a brayer, roll across the image 4–6 times in one direction using medium pressure.

4 Keep negative in contact with fabric for two minutes while keeping both warm by running a hair dryer evenly over the surface, testing the back of the negative with your fingers to monitor heat level. After two minutes, remove negative carefully by peeling back diagonally from one edge.

5 Allow image to dry thoroughly. Trim the fabric to the image. Using a small amount of adhesive, apply the image to the outside of a plain fabric lampshade. Repeat for remaining sides.

VARIATIONS

Embellish the transferred image with fabric paints or dyes, or stain the final fabric print with tea to age. Use larger sheets of fabric decorated with transferred images to make pillows or place mats.

MATERIALS

- developed slide film
- instant slide printer
- Polaroid Type 669, 59, 559, or 809 film
- 100% silk or cotton fabric
- 8" x 10" (20 cm x 25 cm) glass pane
- brayer
- hairdryer
- white craft glue
- plain fabric lampshade
- general craft supplies

TIPS

Peeling the Polaroid negative apart sooner than ten seconds may result in a fogged image. Using heavy pressure to roll the negative with the brayer may distort the image; too little pressure creates white spots on the transfer. Do a few test pieces to acquaint yourself with the process.

A special gift for a mother-to-be, this quilt modernizes the tradition of a sewing bee. Color transfers, created easily at copy shops and reflecting the artistic efforts of a group of friends, are harmonized into one heirloom piece. Copyright-free art, also called "clip art," is a wonderful resource to find ironwork or other designs. Use the same three crayons in varying combinations for each square. Having a group of friends color the squares makes the whole greater than the sum of its parts.

photocopy-transfer
friendship quilt

Makes one quilt

1 Choose twelve ironwork squares from a clip art book, or sketch your own designs. Using a black-and-white photocopying machine, enlarge square to 2 3/4" (7 cm) on each side. Color each square with the same three crayons.

2 Take the completed squares to a copy shop that offers color transfers. Enlarge each design to a 6" (15 cm) square onto transfer paper. Trim each transfer so that there is no more than 1/4" (.25 cm) of white space surrounding each colored design

3 Create a template from grid paper measuring 10 1/2" (27 cm) square, and cut out a 6" (15 cm) square from the center. Cut out twelve 10 1/2" (27 cm) squares from the cotton fabric using the template as a guide. Cover a wood surface with a pillowcase. Place a fabric square face up on the surface, smoothing to remove wrinkles, and position one transfer facedown at the center using the grid-paper template to check placement. Remove the template and iron the transfer to the fabric with a dry iron, moving the iron from edge to edge in a circular motion for a count of thirty, or according to transfer manufacturer's directions. Remove the backing from the transfer by peeling back slowly from one edge. Repeat for remaining squares.

4 Pin completed squares together, three across and four down. Sew with a 1/4" (.5 cm) seam on all edges; press seams open. Cut a 30 1/2" x 40 1/2" (77 cm x 103 cm) section from both the cotton fabric and batting for a backing panel and filling. Pin the right sides of both the front and back fabrics to one another and place batting on top. Sew a 1/4" (.5 cm) seam through all layers around the edge, leaving a 12" (30 cm) opening at the bottom.

5 Turn the blanket right side out. Turn in the edges of the 12" (30 cm) hole and slip-stitch closed. Using white quilting thread and a large needle, tack the points where four corners meet by sewing a single stitch from the front of the quilt through the back of the quilt, then back to the front. Knot and trim thread to 1" (3 cm). Repeat for the remaining five cross sections.

MATERIALS
- copyright-free art
- 3 crayons
- black-and-white and color photocopying machines
- 11" x 17" (28 cm x 43 cm) pad of graph paper
- color copy iron-on transfer sheets
- 4 yards (3.7 m) smooth cotton fabric
- iron
- old pillow case
- quilt batting
- sewing machine
- white quilting thread
- large embroidery needle
- general craft supplies

TIPS
If your copy shop does not stock transfer paper, you can purchase the 8 1/2" x 11" (22 cm x 28 cm) sheets at an office supply store. Most color transfers are machine washable, but refer to the manufacturer's directions for specific washing instructions.

ARTIST: LAURA MCFADDEN

~2000~

Livia & Isaac

Transfers *to Wood*

Wood provides a beautiful, functional, and readily available surface for transfers. Veneers, unfinished wood, and even finished wood can be decorated and enhanced with photos and artwork. There is even specialty veneer on the market that can be safely run through an ordinary ink jet printer. Most fabric-oriented methods of transfer can be used successfully on wood, and the finished project will look fantastic if a few key differences are taken into consideration. The trick to a successful wood transfer is to coordinate the color and grain of the wood with the photo or illustration that is to be transferred. Generally, lighter-colored woods with simple or minimal grain patterns work best when the final image needs to remain as close to the original as possible. Darker or heavily grained woods will modify the image quite a bit, which opens up a whole realm of artistic possibilities that is bound to inspire interesting, expressive projects. When using transparent transfer mediums or papers, the beauty of the wood shows through in all the white areas of an image. This makes the transfer more convincing, and adds depth and sophistication to the project, such as in the frame project on page 44. Seek out wooden surfaces in the home that are in need of refurbishing or decorating, such as end tables, chair backs, or shelves. By carefully selecting the image, transfer method, and surface, it's possible to create pieces that seamlessly blend the art with the object. Sometimes a small accent is all that's needed, and sometimes completely covering a surface is most effective. It's also a good idea to test ideas by trying them out on a piece of scrap wood that closely matches the color and grain of the intended transfer surface. Finally, don't forget to experiment with all kinds of wood as well as different types of artwork.

Techniques and Tips
for Wood Transfers

As with fabrics, there are a variety of transfer methods from which to choose when working with wood. In general, note that softer woods, such as balsa, take transfers more easily and quickly. Harder woods like oak will also work, but the process will take longer. It's also a little trickier, because the transfer can slip and smear once it is heated but not yet fully fused to the wood.

Always begin with finely sanded, unvarnished, unsealed wood. This will ensure that the surface is as porous and smooth as possible, which results in the highest quality transfer. Seal or varnish the project after the transfer has been adhered to protect both the wood and the artwork, but test the finish first. Some heavy-duty or industrial-strength finishes can damage transfers. Acrylic, water-based products are always a safe option.

TRANSFER METHODS

HEAT TRANSFER PAPER
Heat transfer paper is intended for transferring to fabric, but it can be applied to virtually any surface, including wood. To use it successfully on wood, there are a few things to keep in mind. Following are some troubleshooting tips and tricks (for further information on heat transfer paper and how to use it, see page 18).

Tips & Tricks for Heat Transfer Sheets on Wood

- Use gentle pressure and a straight, up-and-down motion to iron transfers in place. The transfer is more malleable and prone to smearing on wood than on fabric, so do not use a circular motion. Opaque transfer sheets are less apt to smear than translucent sheets.

- Translucent heat transfer sheets for copiers are easier to work with on wood than those designed for ink jets, which tend to slip and smear more.

- Use a medium to low heat setting for wood to avoid crazing. The wood will heat up quickly, but it will take longer than with fabric to transfer an image.

- Generally, wait until a transfer has cooled slightly to peel it. Otherwise, it will most likely tear off unevenly unless the wood is very soft, like balsa.

- If an area of the transfer bubbles up or starts to peel after the backing is removed, cover with a piece of the used backing and go over it with very light, quick strokes with an iron.

- Opaque transfer sheets work well with darker or heavily grained woods, because the integrity of the transfer remains intact. Painting around a transfer is another effective way to visually integrate it with the wood. This can soften the edges of the transfer and make it seem as if it has been hand painted.

PRINTABLE WOOD VENEER

This specially treated wood can be used with ink jet printers but not color copiers. It is also fairly expensive, so always print on paper first to check for any problems with artwork, then print on the veneer when the design is finalized. Once printed, it can be used the same way standard veneer would be used—for marquetry and other kinds of inlay, game boards, cards, candle shades, and just about anything else.

Tips & Tricks for Printable Wood Veneer

· Store the veneer in its protective package, and place it under a stack of books to keep it flat.

· Avoid touching the wood's surface before printing. Oils can interfere with the transfer process.

· Let the printed veneer dry for one hour before using it.

· To seal the wood, first use a spray finish to avoid smearing the ink. A brush-on finish can then be applied, if desired.

· Printers usually have a "thick mode" that can be engaged when printing on cardstock or other materials that are thicker than regular paper. Set the printer on this mode when using veneer.

· Load only one sheet of veneer at a time and no other papers. It's a good idea to load and eject a sheet before printing to check for any problems.

· If the edges of the veneer are damaged, this could interfere with the printer's ability to grab the sheet. Simply trim it to create a new, perfect edge, and keep in mind that there will be less space to print on when designing the transfer.

· This material is very absorbent, so fine lines have a tendency to bleed. Using a lot of ink, then, creates a blurry image. In general, try to use the least amount of ink possible to obtain acceptable results. Higher printing resolutions yield more detailed images, but they also use more ink. Try to find a balance between the two.

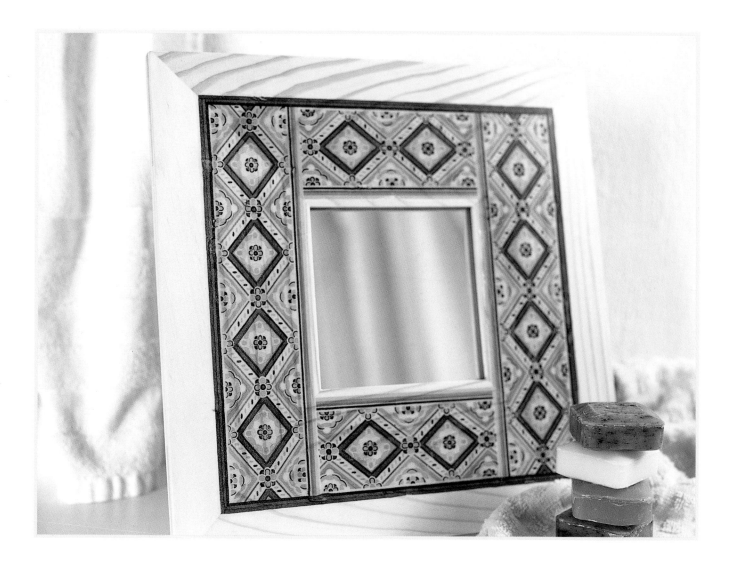

Border-Framed *Mirror*

This wide-edged frame is perfect for a transfer project because it offers a lot of room for artwork. Jazz up a plain, ordinary frame with a pretty, detailed border. There is a multitude of clip art books that offer an array of styles and colors from which to choose. The straight edges of the border here were a cinch to cut, but more intricate designs are well worth the effort. Both finished and unfinished frames will take transfers. Unfinished wood is easier to work with because the surface is more absorbent, but be sure to apply any paint or stains before adhering the transfer for a cleaner result. Before applying a transfer over a slick finish, do a test on the back of the object to make sure the result is acceptable. See page 42 for tips.

MATERIALS

- *wooden frame*

- *heat transfer paper*

- *tape*

- *craft knife or scissors*

- *iron*

- *ruler*

- *cutting mat*

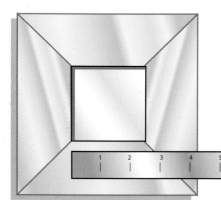

Starting *Out*

Do a test transfer on a piece of scrap wood of the same type as the frame before beginning the project to determine the optimal heat setting for the iron. The setting will vary from one brand of transfer paper to another. The art for these projects can be found on page 284.

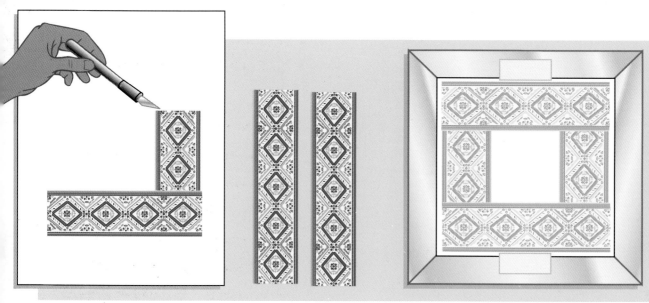

STEP 1

Prepare the transfer. Measure the frame to determine the size that the border needs to be. Then, scan or make four photocopies of the artwork at the necessary percentage. Create a continuous border by piecing together four strips of the artwork; this can be done by hand or on a computer. Next, photocopy the prepared artwork to a heat transfer sheet for color copiers by following the manufacturer's instructions.

STEP 2

Cut the transfer out. Use scissors or a craft knife, a cutting mat, and a ruler, and leave $1/16$"–$1/8$" (1.5 mm–3 mm) around the artwork. Next, use small pieces of tape to secure the two opposite sides of the transfer. This will help prevent it from sliding around the surface of the wood. Try to tape only the outer $1/16$"–$1/8$" (1.5 mm–3 mm) border of the transfer.

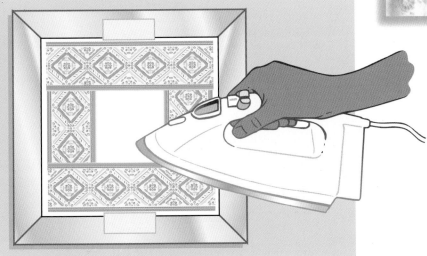

STEP 3

Iron the transfer in place. A medium to low heat setting works
well for a finely finished wooden surface. Use a straight up-and-
down motion when ironing rather than a side-to-side or circular
motion, to prevent the image from smearing. It should take only
a minute or two to complete the transfer. Let the transfer cool
before peeling it off to ensure a complete transfer.

Variation:

Try adding a few smaller transfers to
an unfinished wooden frame for quick
accents. The black-and-white illustrations
used here were colored with pencils before they were copied to a piece of heat
transfer paper. To prepare the frame, coat
it with translucent, white water-based
wood stain and let it dry completely.
Then, iron the transfers in place. It is not
necessary to tape the transfer to secure it
if the iron will cover all or most of the
image at once. Finally, coat the frame
with a colored water-based wood stain,
if desired. Don't worry if some of the
stain gets on the images, because it
can be easily wiped away.

Illustrated *End Table*

The art nouveau-style illustration on this tabletop is surrounded by a painted border and stained wood for a matted, framed look. The painted border also helps to visually integrate the transfer with the surface of the table, while staining the other areas calls attention to the beauty of the wood. Pairing these decorating techniques creates the illusion of hand painting. This is especially the effect when opaque transfer paper is used, because detailed images are less apt to become muddled or obscured by inconsistencies or dark knots in the wood. Try refurbishing antiqued furniture with a few transfers, but leave the distressed finish intact.

MATERIALS

- *unfinished wooden table*
- *green pickling gel or water-based stain*
- *acrylic paint*
- *acrylic varnish*
- *opaque heat transfer paper*
- *craft knife*
- *sponge applicator brush*
- *ruler*
- *iron*
- *pencil*
- *masking tape*

Starting *Out*

Use masking tape for clean, crisp lines when painting the border. Don't worry about a clean inner edge, though, because the transfer will cover it. The art for this project can be found on page 286.

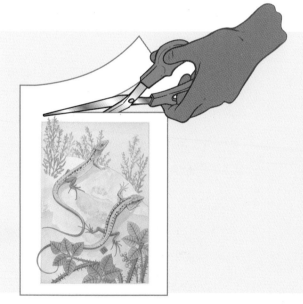

STEP 1

Prepare and print out artwork. Measure the tabletop to determine the how large the artwork needs to be. Then, photocopy or print artwork onto an opaque heat transfer sheet following the manufacturer's instructions. Leave the paper backing on the transfer and carefully trim around the tail and flowers that extend past the border of the art using a craft knife and cutting mat.

STEP 2

Stain and paint the table. First, mark the desired position of the artwork on the tabletop with a pencil and ruler. Then, measure and mark a border around the area to use as a painting guideline. Next, apply a water-based stain or pickling gel to the table with a sponge applicator brush, leaving the space for the artwork and painted border untouched. Cactus green pickling gel by Delta was used here. Once the stain is dry, paint the border with opaque acrylic paint.

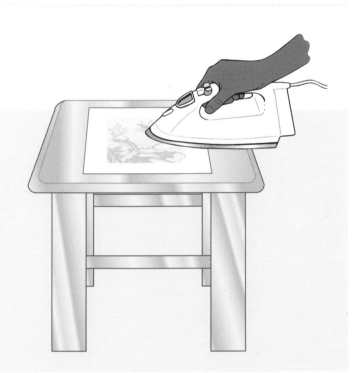

STEP 3

<u>Iron transfer in place</u>. Preheat the iron on a medium heat setting. Peel the backing off the transfer and position the transfer on the table. Place the silicon pressing sheet over the transfer and use a circular motion and gentle pressure to adhere the transfer. This should only take a few minutes. Be sure all the edges of the transfer are secure. Once the transfer has cooled, finish the table with two or three coats of acrylic varnish.

Variation:

Try decorating the sides or the legs of a table instead of the top for a more understated look. Follow the directions for the main project, but completely paint and stain the table before applying the transfers. A white transparent stain was used for the tabletop, and the remaining areas were painted. Remember to mark pencil guidelines for each transfer to help in positioning. The art for this project can be found on page 287.

Faux-Painted *Clock*

The graphic, stylized floral design on this clock is reminiscent of the decorative folk painting often seen on wooden furniture. Simple, solid clip art like this is typically black to begin with, but solid colors can easily be changed. Even a basic image-editing program will have color-manipulation capabilities. If creating artwork using a copier, simply ask the clerk to change the hue. The monochromatic color scheme makes the clock easier to read, and it is easy to create with transparent transfer paper. As long as the transfer color is similar to the stain, the colors will merge and match well.

MATERIALS

- *unfinished wooden clock kit*

- *wood stain*

- *acrylic varnish*

- *heat transfer paper*

- *craft knife*

- *cutting mat*

- *sponge applicator brush*

- *fine sandpaper*

- *lint-free rag, such as a T-shirt*

- *iron*

Starting *Out*

Unfinished wooden clocks kits come with a movement and hardware and are very easy to assemble. Be sure to check if the clock hands are included or not. See *Resources* on page 298 for information. The art for this project and the variation can be found on pages 286 and 287.

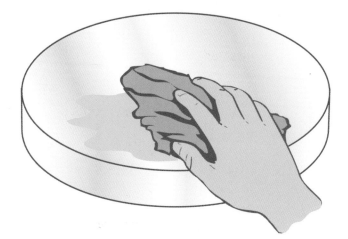

STEP 1

Stain the clock face. First, smooth out any rough spots with fine sandpaper. Remove all dust with a damp rag. Then, apply the wood stain. Purple oil-based wood stain mixed with an equal amount of white wood stain was used here to create a lavender patina. The clock face was also treated with an extra layer of pure white stain to make it a little lighter than the beveled edge. Wait at least twenty-four hours for the stain to dry before applying the transfer or it will be difficult to adhere.

STEP 2

Prepare the artwork. Measure the clock face to determine how large the artwork needs to be. Then, photocopy or print the artwork to a heat transfer sheet, following the manufacturer's instructions. Trim the artwork, removing as much of the white areas as possible.

[Tip:]

Oil-based wood stains take at least a day to dry completely, but their advantages are greater control and a finer finish. They are best applied with a lint-free rag, which eliminates the need to clean brushes with harsh solvents.

STEP 3

Iron the transfer in place. Preheat the iron on a low to medium heat setting. Use a straight up-and-down motion when ironing, rather than a side-to-side or circular motion, to prevent the image from smearing. This should only take a few minutes. Be sure all the edges of the transfer are secure, and check frequently to see if they are adhered. Let the transfer cool completely before peeling the backing paper off. Use a craft knife to cut the center of the transfer out, where the hole for the clock movement is located. Then, finish the clock with one or two coats of acrylic varnish. Once dry, attach the movement and hands to the clock face according to the package instructions.

Variation:

Try whitewashing wood to even out the variations when using intricate patterns. Some of the wood grain will still show through, but the transfer will remain distinct. A layer of white water-based wood stain, which dries in a few minutes, was applied to this clock. Be sure to apply this type of stain quickly and evenly. To determine the correct placement of the numbers for a clock face, use graph paper to easily but precisely divide the area into twelve segments, like a pie.

Georgetta D'Mario

Livia McRee

Isaac Stone

Family *Tree*

This family tree is easily updated anytime there is a marriage or birth, because the photographic panels are a snap to make using inexpensive, easy-to-cut balsa wood. Arrange the panels on a wall to visually suggest a tree, or lay them out in a traditional genealogical pattern. Skeletonized leaves can be used in many ways to accent the panels and are available in several colors at craft and art supply stores. Also try using pressed foliage or flowers. To add names, first print them out from a word processing program, then have them reversed and copied to a heat transfer sheet at a copy shop.

MATERIALS

- *balsa wood planks*

- *skeletonized leaves*

- *decorative papers*

- *white pickling gel or water-based stain*

- *heat transfer paper*

- *craft knife*

- *cutting mat*

- *glue stick*

- *sponge applicator brush*

- *fine sandpaper*

- *iron*

Starting *Out*

Use a glue stick to quickly and easily adhere the paper and leaves to the photo panels.

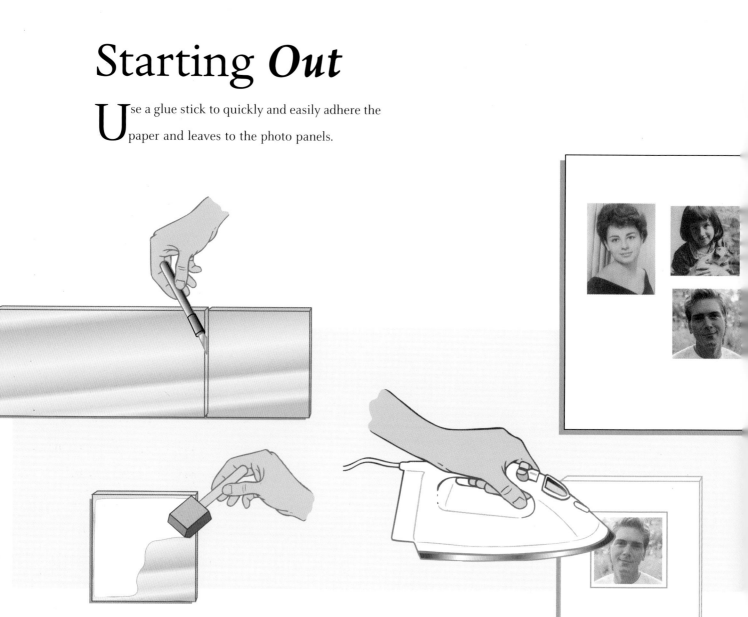

STEP 1

<u>Cut and stain the panels</u>. Cut the balsa wood planks into squares or rectangles. The ones here are 6" x 6" (15 cm x 15 cm) and 6" x 7" (15 cm x 18 cm). Smooth the cut edges with fine sandpaper. Then, apply a transparent white wash to the panels with a sponge applicator brush. Let them dry thoroughly for several hours or overnight; any moisture in the wood will prevent the transfers from adhering properly.

STEP 2

<u>Prepare and iron the transfers in place</u>. Compile the photographs to be used, then size them using a color copier or a computer. Photocopy or print artwork onto a heat transfer sheet, following the manufacturer's instructions. Fit as many as possible on each sheet. Carefully trim around each photo using scissors or a craft knife and cutting mat. Next, preheat the iron on a low to medium heat setting. Adhere the transfers to the centers of the panels. Use a straight up-and-down motion when ironing, rather than a side-to-side or circular motion, to prevent the image from smearing. This should only take a few minutes. Check adhesion frequently as you iron, and be sure all the edges of the transfers are secure. Let the transfers cool completely before peeling the backing paper off.

Variation:

Make panels to celebrate and commemorate special occasions, such as a special anniversary, family reunion, or graduation. Silver-coated leaves and metallic papers were used to complement the black-and-white photograph used here.

STEP 3

<u>Decorate the panels with leaves and paper</u>. Arrange and adhere the leaves as desired on the panels. Then, measure and cut squares of paper that are $1/2$" (4 cm) larger all around than the transfers. Cut out the centers of these paper squares to create a $1/4$" (5 mm) border for the transferred photographs. Position them over the transfers and adhere to the panel. To cover the edges of the panels, cut 6" (15 cm) strips; determine how wide the strips should be by measuring the thickness of the wood, then add $1/2$" (1 cm). This will ensure a $1/4$" (5 mm) border around the front and back of the panel. Lightly score the strips lengthwise, $1/4$" (5 mm) in from both sides, using a craft knife. Fold the strips in to a *U* shape and adhere them to the edges of the panels. Finish the panels with a coat of water-based acrylic varnish, if desired.

Transfers *to Stone and Porous Surfaces*

Transfers can be applied to virtually any porous surface, which opens up an exciting realm of possibilities for the crafter. Terra-cotta, marble, plaster, stone—all these materials can be transformed with artwork and photos. From flowerpots to marble coasters, decorated clay and stone can be incorporated into the home with ease. Use plaster or other casting materials for custom-made surfaces ranging from molding boxes, frames, and ornaments, to just about anything else. The four projects in this section are merely a starting point and are intended to be an inspiring introduction to this fun way of crafting with images. When working with hard, porous surfaces, there are two important differences in the transfer process to keep in mind. Most importantly, it will take a longer time to adhere the transfer. In order for proper fusing to take place, the entire surface must be thoroughly heated—something that is more quickly achieved when using fabrics and wood. Also, once heated, the whole object will usually retain this heat for several minutes, especially stone surfaces, so wear protective gloves. Also, it may be difficult to get a complete transfer when a hard surface is bumpy or fairly uneven, since there is no give as there is with fabric and even wood. Try sanding the surface, if possible, or avoiding areas with pits or chips. Explore the variety of materials available at home-improvement centers and tile stores, because these places are sure to be full of potential craft projects. As long as a surface is fairly smooth and fairly porous, there's sure to be way to decorate it with transfers. It's easiest to transfer to a flat surface, but even rounded surfaces can work, so don't be intimidated by them. Finally, experiment with anything and everything—there's always a new technique waiting to be discovered.

Techniques and Tips *for Stone and Porous Surface Transfers*

The materials used in this chapter—stone, marble, plaster, and ceramics—come in many different colors and textures. Usually, these raw materials are sold for a particular use, but don't let that be a limitation. Flooring tiles, when backed with cork, make great coasters; garden slate, fitted with hanging hardware, can be used as a plaque; and inexpensive terra-cotta pots can be broken apart, decorated, and used in a mosaic.

After completing a few transfer projects, it will be easy to determine what types of surfaces will work. In general, flat, smooth, and porous surfaces are ideal. Curved surfaces are more difficult, but not impossible to transfer to. Nonporous materials like glass and metal could be used, but a much higher heat, such as that of a kiln, is needed for a successful transfer.

While no specific products exist—yet—for transferring to these types of surfaces, beautiful, durable, easy transfers are possible. Don't be afraid to improvise or use a standard technique in a new way. This often leads to surprising, satisfying results. As you get to know the different transfer methods and products available, it will become easier and easier to predict how a certain one will work on a given surface.

TRANSFER METHODS

HEAT TRANSFER PAPER

Both opaque and translucent heat transfer sheets can be ironed on stone and porous surfaces. Opaque transfers are very useful for medium- to dark-colored surfaces, such as terra-cotta and slate. See page 18 for a discussion of heat transfer paper and how to use it, but refer to the tips and tricks listed here for troubleshooting when working with the stone and porous materials used in this chapter.

Tips & Tricks for Stone and Marble Transfers

- For stone and marble, preheat the iron on high. It will take several minutes to complete the transfer, because the entire stone needs to become hot before the image will bond to it.

- Tack down the center of the transfer using firm up-and-down-pressure. Once it is stationary, vigorously iron the image using a circular motion.

- The image is only prone to smearing once the stone is completely heated, but at this point, the transfer should be complete. Check the progress frequently by using a craft knife or similar tool to lift up a corner of the transfer.

- Wear protective gloves when working with stone and marble, because they will become very hot during the transfer process. Also work on an appropriate surface that won't be damaged by the heat.

- For a finish ranging from matte to satin, peel the transfer backing off slowly, once it has cooled off enough to handle. For a glossier finish, wait for the transfer to cool completely before peeling.

- If there are any pieces of the transfer left on the backing, stop peeling and press it back into place. Then, reheat the area and let it cool completely.

- Sometimes, stone surfaces will have chips, cracks, or nicks. The transfer won't adhere to these areas that dip below the surface. Sometimes, this enhances the design by giving it an antique look. To fill the cracks for an even surface, use nonsanded white grout. Tint premixed grout with acrylic paint or grout powder with dry paint pigments.

Tips & Tricks for Ceramic Transfers

- Preheat the iron and set it on high, as with stone and marble. It will take several minutes to complete the transfer as well. Be sure to iron vigorously in a circular motion once the transfer is tacked down.

- Use only unglazed pottery, such as classic terra-cotta pots or bisqueware. Unglazed pottery will have a matte, chalky finish. Bisque is low-fired, usually white, and comes in a variety of forms, such as frames and vases. Purchase it from paint-it-yourself pottery studios or ceramic suppliers.

- Use coarse sandpaper to smooth any bumps, or use an industrial metal file for large bumps.

- Sponge off ceramic surfaces and let them dry completely before transferring. There is usually dust and fine clay residue on the surface of unglazed pottery. It may take several washings to get the surface totally clean.

- Since ceramics such as terra-cotta are dark, images on translucent heat transfer paper will be significantly modified by the color of the clay. A photograph, for example, will create a subtle pattern that appears to have faded over time. Dark, solid line images will create a stronger, more obvious pattern.

- To preserve the functionality of such an item as a flowerpot, seal the entire surface, including the interior. Unglazed ceramics are very absorbent, and contact with water will eventually damage transfers.

Tips & Tricks for Plaster Transfers

- Preheat the iron on a medium setting. It will take several minutes to complete the transfer, but if it isn't adhering well, turn the heat to high and iron more firmly and vigorously.

- There are many premade plaster shapes and forms available, which makes this material ideal for experimentation.

- Plaster objects are easy to make from scratch; simply measure out a portion of the dry mix, and slowly add water until a pancake batter consistency is achieved.

- Experiment with premade molds, or improvised forms such as cardboard boxes.

- Try tinting plaster with dry paint pigments before adding water.

Stone *Tile Coasters*

Artificial stone tiles, such as the ones used here, are inexpensive and are available at most home-improvement stores. Choose tiles with a smooth, evenly colored surface with a few hairline cracks or other imperfections for an antique, mural-like effect. Be sure the tiles are unglazed but highly polished, which creates an absorbent, smooth surface that is perfect for transfers. The vintage advertisements on these coasters might have been painted on a pub or restaurant wall, and using the transparent heat transfer method replicates this effect. And since heat transfers are designed to be functional fabric embellishments, they stand up well to hot drinks, moisture, and washing.

MATERIALS

- *4" (10 cm) stone tiles*

- *heat transfer paper*

- *cork or felt*

- *craft knife or scissors*

- *ruler*

- *cutting mat*

- *iron*

- *oven mitts*

- *permanent glue*

Starting *Out*

Stone tiles will heat up quickly when ironed, so wear oven mitts and be careful when handling them. The art for this project can be found on page 289.

STEP 1

Prepare and print out artwork. Select the artwork and determine the size it needs to be to fit the coasters. Square transfers will work best. Next, photocopy or print artwork to a heat transfer sheet, following the manufacturer's instructions. Be sure to flip the image if there is type so that it will read correctly when transferred.

STEP 2

Cut the transfers out. Use scissors or a craft knife, cutting mat, and ruler. Leave an 1/8" (3 mm) border around the artwork.

STEP 3

<u>Iron the transfers in place</u>. Follow the manufacturer's directions. A high heat setting works best for stone surfaces. Tack the center down first, then the edges. It will take several minutes to complete the transfer. Keep checking the edges to see if they have been completely transferred. Finally, adhere cork or felt to the back of each tile with permanent glue.

Variation:

These classic architectural illustrations are a perfect fit for white marble coasters. Black-and-white art works best with the grayish streaks that run through this stone, which otherwise tends to muddy and obscure color images. To work with marble, just follow the directions for the main project. The art for this project can be found on page 290.

Faux Porcelain *Plaster Box*

These plaster boxes can be made quickly and inexpensively using premade molds, but many household objects, such as Tupperware and cardboard boxes, can be used as molds too. The pure white, claylike finish of plaster can be used to convincingly replicate the look of porcelain. When combined with a blue and white Chinese pattern, the result is reminiscent of traditional decorative pottery. Translucent heat transfer paper fuses perfectly with plaster, while preserving the inherent, subtle tonal variations that add a realistic touch to the finished project. Try adding thin layers of high-gloss varnish until the box takes on a glazed look. Let each coat dry completely before applying the next for the most effective sheen.

MATERIALS

- *Quick-drying craft plaster*
- *heart box mold*
- *silver acrylic paint*
- *acrylic varnish*
- *heat transfer paper*
- *scissors*
- *sponge applicator brush*
- *paintbrush*
- *iron*

Starting *Out*

A wash of silver acrylic paint thinned with water was used on the edges and sides of this box for a subtle antique finish. Use silver foil sheets for a shiny, pure metallic look. The art for these projects can be found on page 290.

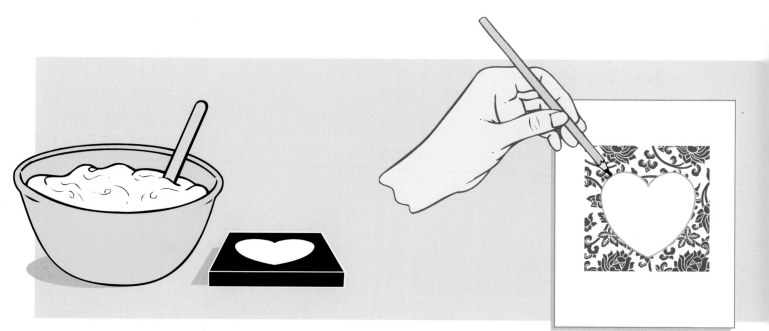

STEP 1

<u>Make the plaster box</u>. Following the manufacturer's directions, mix water into the plaster slowly until a consistency like that of pancake batter is achieved. Use a disposable container and a wooden stick. Then, pour the mixture into the mold and tap around the edges to bring air bubbles to the surface. Make sure the mold is on a level surface. Let it dry for about thirty minutes, until it is firm to the touch but still cool and damp. Then, remove the box and lid from the mold and either air dry for twenty-four hours or quick-dry using a microwave according to the manufacturer's instructions. Paint the sides and edges of the box if desired.

STEP 2

<u>Prepare the artwork</u>. Photocopy or print artwork onto a heat transfer sheet following the manufacturer's instructions. Make sure the artwork will be big enough to cover the box lid. Then, trace the box lid shape on the back of the transfer using a pencil (the outline of the artwork should still be visible). Cut along the traced line with scissors.

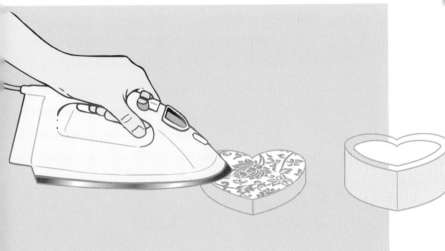

STEP 3

<u>Iron the transfers in place</u>. Preheat the iron on a medium to high heat setting. Place the transfer face down on the box lid and iron using a circular motion and firm pressure to tack it down. Once it is in place, continue ironing it until it is completely adhered, using gentle pressure to avoid smearing it. This should take several minutes. Once cooled, peel away the paper. Finally, finish the entire box with one or two coats of acrylic varnish using a sponge applicator brush.

Variation:

An ornate transfer can transform a simple, plain container into a treasure box, perfect for gift giving or storing precious jewelry. Size a square piece of art to fit perfectly on the lid, and follow the directions for the main project. (Plaid makes several different kinds of molds for plaster, including the square design seen here. See *Resources,* page 298, for further information.)

Terra-Cotta *Pots*

Unglazed terra-cotta makes an interesting, practical surface for transfers. When selecting pots, keep in mind that the smoother they are, the easier it will be to transfer images. The flat, angled sides of this pot made the transfer process even easier, and the rectangular shape of each side lends an Egyptian air to the project. Delineating the top, bottom, and each side edge accentuates the cartouche effect. This design can be translated to any pot by simply painting rectangular borders around a stack of three or more transfers like the bird used here.

MATERIALS

- *unglazed terra-cotta pots*

- *yellow ochre acrylic paint*

- *acrylic varnish*

- *opaque heat transfer paper with silicon pressing sheet*

- *craft knife*

- *cutting mat*

- *sponge applicator brush*

- *paintbrush*

- *iron*

Starting *Out*

Opaque transfer paper takes easily to the often rough, rounded, and uneven surface of terra-cotta. Sealing the pot's exterior with varnish makes it a functional piece, but to further protect the transfers from moisture, coat the inside as well with terra-cotta tile sealer (available at home centers). The art for these projects can be found on page 291.

STEP 1

Prepare and cut the transfers out. Determine how many images will be needed to decorate the pot. Then, photocopy or print the artwork onto an opaque heat transfer sheet following the manufacturer's instructions. Fit as much artwork as possible on each sheet. Using scissors or a craft knife, a cutting mat, and a ruler, cut as close to the artwork as possible, without cutting into it. Leave the backing paper on while cutting.

STEP 2

Prepare and paint the pot. To prepare the pot, use a damp sponge to wipe away all dust and dirt. Then, add painted accents if desired. The edges of this octagonal pot were delineated to accentuate the vertical, Egyptian-inspired design.

STEP 3

Iron the transfers in place. Preheat the iron on a medium to high heat setting. Peel the backing off one of the transfers and position it on the pot. Next, place the silicon pressing sheet over the transfer and iron using a circular motion and gentle pressure to adhere the transfer. This should only take a few minutes. Be sure all the edges of the transfer are secure. Repeat with the rest of the transfers. Once the pot has cooled, finish the pot with one or two coats of acrylic varnish using a sponge applicator brush.

Variation:

A quick accent, like this floral artwork, is a fast and satisfying way to enhance ordinary pots. Try making several pots and placing them in a row along a sunny windowsill. Opaque transfer paper is the best choice for this project, because, unlike transparent transfer paper, it adheres well to rounded surfaces. Follow the directions for the main project to make these pots. Because they are round, however, they will need to be held stationary to keep them from rolling around while ironing the transfers in place. So be sure to wear an oven mitt on one hand.

Saltillo *House Number Plaque*

Made in Mexico, Saltillo clay tiles are similar to terra-cotta, but they have beautiful yellow, orange, and tan variegations—no two are alike. They are available from home-improvement centers and stores specializing in tile and flooring materials. The friendly sun pattern here accentuates the warm feeling of the tile and gives the project a south-of-the-border flair. The color of the artwork can be easily adjusted to suit a particular color scheme; try repeating a smaller version of the design in a very light color to create a more subtle background pattern.

MATERIALS

- *unglazed Saltillo tiles*

- *light yellow acrylic paint*

- *opaque heat transfer paper*

- *outdoor acrylic varnish*

- *craft knife*

- *cutting mat*

- *sponge applicator brush*

- *paintbrush*

- *iron*

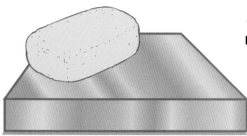

Starting *Out*

This plaque can be hung several ways. Try mirror clips or framing the entire tile in wood. A drill fitted with a masonry bit can also be used to make nail holes in the back of the tile. The art for these projects can be found on page 292.

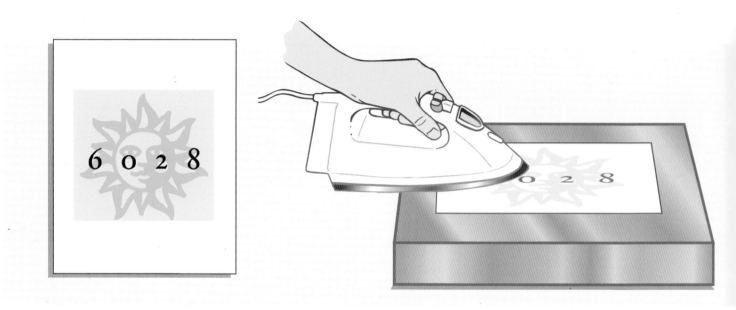

STEP 1

Prepare the artwork and the tile. Scan or copy the background to the desired size, and adjust the hue if desired. Then, choose a computer font for the house number. Some image-editing programs have typesetting capabilities. The type can also be set in a word processing program, then printed, scanned, and incorporated into the artwork as an image (see page 14, *Modifying Art by Hand and Computer*). Next, photocopy or print artwork onto an opaque heat transfer sheet following the manufacturer's instructions. To prepare the tile, use a damp sponge to wipe away all dust and dirt. Make sure the tile is completely dry before applying the transfer.

STEP 2

Cut the transfer out and iron it in place. Use a craft knife, cutting mat, and ruler. Cut as close to the artwork as possible without cutting into it. Leave the backing paper on while cutting. Preheat the iron on a medium to high heat setting. Peel the backing off the transfer and center it on the tile. Next, place the silicon pressing sheet over the transfer and with an iron use a circular motion and gentle pressure to adhere the transfer. This should only take a few minutes. Be sure all the edges of the transfer are secure.

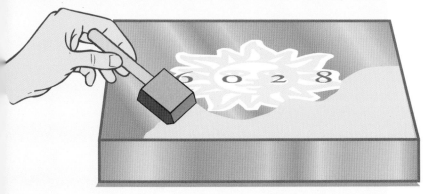

STEP 3

<u>Antique and seal the plaque</u>. Combine one part of the yellow paint to two parts varnish to make a glazing medium. Apply the mixture with a sponge brush applicator over the whole tile for a sun-bleached look. Finally, finish the tile with several coats of acrylic varnish for outdoor use. Be sure to completely seal the tile for durability.

Variation:

Try using a full-color photo of the house, and superimpose the numbers on top as described in the main project. Rather than antiquing the entire plaque with a glaze, the photo seen here was lightened digitally to give it a softer look, which also helps to make the numbers pop. A color copier can also be used to lighten photos (see page 14, *Modifying Art by Hand and Computer*). Follow the directions for transferring the photo and sealing the plaque as described in the main project.

IMAGE TRANSFER
album

Display a favorite photograph using this unusual technique that transfers an image onto foil. This album features a quiet and sophisticated design, allowing it to fit into any decorating style.

MATERIALS	

• 4 sheets of silver-colored foil
• Sheet of decal medium
• Xyron machine with adhesive-
  only cartridge
• Photo album
	• Chipboard or noncorrugated
	  cardboard
	• Scissors
	• Favorite photo

1. Apply adhesive to the back of three sheets silver foil using the Xyron machine. Cover the front, spine, and back of the photo album with the silver foil.

2. Photocopy a favorite photo onto the decal medium, following the manufacturer's directions. Transfer the photo decal to the remaining sheet of silver foil. Allow it to dry and cure completely.

3. Apply adhesive to the back of the sheet of silver foil with photo decal.

4. Using the scissors, trim the chipboard to the same size as the photo album. Cover the chipboard with the photo decal.

5. Apply adhesive to the back of the covered chipboard, and mount it on the front of the photo album.

Artist: Beth Wheeler

Vista
Studio
Martinsville, Ind.

Transfers *to Polymer Clay*

Polymer clay is a versatile and inexpensive modeling material that readily takes transfers of many kinds. Available at craft-supply stores, it can be shaped easily and is then cured to a durable hardness in a home oven. There are many polymer clay tools and companion products, such as extruders to push molds, which make working with the clay even easier and more exciting. All the standard transfer techniques can be applied to polymer clay, but this popular material has special properties that allow for even more ways to transfer images. Indeed, polymer clay is a material that sparks a lot of creativity and experimentation in those who are intrigued by its versatility. Black-and-white photocopies can be directly transferred to raw clay—no medium involved. Enhance the photocopy with colored pencils, and the pigments will also bake into the clay to create a permanent transfer. Also available is a liquid transfer medium called Liquid Sculpey, which can be used as a transfer medium with photocopies or be used to create decals that are applied to raw clay (see *Resources* on page 298). Polymer clay is available in a wide variety of colors, but use white, translucent, or lighter varieties when it is important to retain the color of the artwork or photo. Even so, there are many colors to choose from, including gorgeous pearlescent pastels. The many different colors, tools, and techniques of polymer clay craft are enticing, because there are so many possibilities for creating new and unique projects, from translucent suncatchers to decals that can be applied a to variety of surfaces. And with its flexibility to mold into anything, this is a perfect surface for transferring a treasured photo or a favorite illustration that can be created in an hour or less.

Techniques and Tips
for Polymer Clay Transfers

Polymer clay is simple to use, but there are a few things to keep in mind that will make the process even easier and more successful. First, work on a totally clean surface free of lint, oil, or dust. This debris will be picked up by the clay and is not only unattractive but also can cause incomplete transfers. Wear latex gloves to further prevent the clay from becoming soiled or oily. It's also a good idea to have a baking sheet set aside specifically for polymer clay. Though it is a nontoxic material, it's best not to reuse equipment used for curing clay to prepare food.

The projects in this section involve rolling out the clay to flatten it, which provides the ideal surface for transfers. In order to keep the thickness of the clay consistent, use craft wood sticks that are as thick as the clay needs to be. Simply tape them to the sides of the baking sheet and make sure the rolling pin's edges rest on the sticks while the clay is being flattened in the middle. Wood sticks are available in a variety of thickness at craft and hobby shops, from $1/16$" (1.5 mm) to $1/4$" (5 mm) and even thicker.

Finally, one essential tool for polymer clay crafting is the tissue blade, which is an extremely sharp, thin tool that makes cutting much easier. Tissue blades don't pull or push the clay as they cut, so the result is a nice, clean edge. Be sure to cut the clay once it's had a chance to firm up after the necessary initial kneading and shaping. Craft knives with new blades will also work well, but are much smaller than tissue blades, so more cuts will be needed to do the same amount of work.

TRANSFER METHODS

HEAT TRANSFER PAPER
Both opaque and translucent heat transfer sheets can be used on polymer clay. Both can be ironed on or baked on raw clay. See page 16 for a discussion of heat transfer paper and how to use it, but refer to the tips and tricks listed here for troubleshooting when working with polymer clay.

Tips & Tricks for Heat Transfer Sheets on Polymer Clay

- Place translucent transfers face up on the baking sheet, then put the raw clay shape over it. This helps the transfer adhere evenly and keeps it from buckling up during the baking process.

- Burnish translucent transfers with the back of a spoon after taking them out of the oven to ensure a good bond. Then, wait for the clay to cool completely before removing the backing.

- Opaque transfers can be baked on top of clay, rather than underneath, because they will stick firmly to the raw clay.

- Opaque transfers can also be applied to clay right after baking, when it is still hot.

- Do not bake the transfers more than once or longer than required to cure the clay, because they will start to shrink and crack.

DIRECT PAPER TRANSFERS

Photocopies can be applied face down on raw polymer clay, then baked. Black-and-white copies made from a black-and-white copier work best. When a color copy is used, only part of the ink transfers, resulting in very different colors. For example, black from a color copy machine can result in a rose color. This can lead to some interesting effects, but for truer color, enhance a black-and-white copy with good quality color pencils.

Tips & Tricks for Direct Paper Transfers on Polymer Clay

- In addition to photocopies, printouts from laser printers can also be used to make transfers, but those from ink jet printers cannot.

- The copy should be fairly dark to ensure a rich, solid transfer.

- If the transfer isn't working well or is coming out too light, try another copy machine or change the toner in the laser printer.

- Once the transfer is in place, try not to move the clay or the paper, because this can cause the image to smear. For this reason, it's best to work directly on a baking sheet.

- To create a transfer for a round surface, follow the normal procedure for flat surfaces, but leave the transfer on the clay for fifteen minutes, and don't bake it. Be sure to burnish it well. Then, remove the paper, carefully mold the clay into the rounded shape, and, finally, bake it. This is a great method for making beads.

LIQUID POLYMER TRANSFER MEDIUM

Liquid polymer transfer medium is available in transparent and opaque formulas. Any type of photocopy can be used to make a liquid polymer transfer, and they can be enhanced with color pencils. Just brush a layer of the medium directly on the image, then bake according to the manufacturer's directions. The resulting decal can then be peeled off the paper and used in a number of ways. To transfer to raw clay, just coat the clay with the medium and place the paper transfer on top, then bake as usual. (For information on availability see Polymer Products in *Resources* on page 298.)

Tips & Tricks for Liquid Polymer Transfer Medium

- Ink jet printouts made using standard or multipurpose paper will not create a transfer. However, using photo-quality, matte finish ink jet paper will create a perfect transfer with colors more vibrant than a color copy transfer.

- If the transfer is coming out too faint, try making a color or black-and-white copy darker, using a more brightly colored or darker image, or using a different copy machine altogether.

- Add color to the medium by mixing it with oil paints or dry pigment powders. Acrylic paint, which is water based, will create a bumpy texture during baking when the water boils off.

- After baking, if the transfer is hard to peel off, soak it in some water. The decal will not be damaged.

- When transferring directly to raw clay, be sure there are no air bubbles caught between the paper and the medium. Burnish the transfer with the back of a spoon, and wait until all the paper darkens. This indicates that the medium has soaked in thoroughly.

- The medium can be used as an adhesive to bond raw clay to raw clay, or raw clay to baked clay. Use only a thin coat to attach the pieces, then bake them. Too much medium will cause the pieces to slip and slide.

Pendant and Pin *Set*

This jewelry is made using photo copies of black-and-white illustrations and faux-stone polymer clay. The simulated rose quartz, jade, and turquoise clay featured here are just a few of the styles of specialty clays available. Only simple jewelry-making techniques and minimal supplies are needed to assemble the necklace and pin. Just check the bead and findings section of any craft-supply store. Try using a black-and-white photo and transfer it to brightly colored clay for a fun, contemporary necklace. Or, use miniature cookie cutters to create pendants with interesting shapes.

MATERIALS

- *polymer clay*

- *jump ring*

- *necklace chain*

- *pin backing*

- *silver paint*

- *1/4" (5 mm) thick craft wood strips, at least 12" (30 cm) long*

- *rolling pin*

- *cookie sheet*

- *sharp craft knife or tissue blade*

- *pliers*

- *eye pin*

- *varnish*

- *permanent adhesive*

- *small paintbrush*

- *fine sandpaper*

Starting *Out*

It's best to use black-and-white copies for this project. Color copies create pale transfers, and the final color of the transfer will be completely off from the original. The art for these projects can be found on page 293.

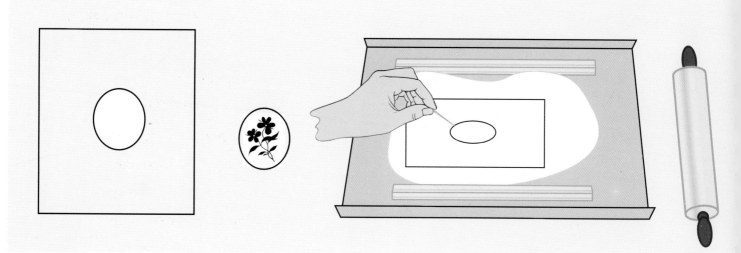

STEP 1

Prepare the artwork. Cut an oval or other shape from a piece of white paper to make a template of the pendant and pin shape and size. Lay it over the image to be used, then determine if the image needs to be enlarged or reduced to better fit the space. Photocopy the image at the appropriate percentage on a black-and-white copier, then cut out the image. Reverse the image when copying it, if desired.

STEP 2

Shape and bake the polymer clay. Knead a small handful of clay until it is softened and very pliable. Place the 1/4" (5 mm) wood strips on the cookie sheet so that the rolling pin rests on them and there is ample space in between to roll out the clay. When the clay is 1/4" (5 mm) thick, place the paper template on top and gently trace the outline into the clay with a craft knife, toothpick, or similar tool. Then, remove the template and carefully cut out the pendant shape with a tissue blade or sharp craft knife. Next, lay the photocopied image face down on the clay. Press it gently into the clay by going over it with the rolling pin once. Rub the edges gently to smooth them out, then stick an eye pin into the top of the pendant. Follow the same procedure to make the pin, but don't add an eye pin. Bake the clay on the cookie sheet following the manufacturer's directions, generally fifteen minutes per 1/4" (5 mm) of thickness at 275 degrees Fahrenheit (135 degrees Celsius).

[Tip:]

To attach the pendant to the chain, use jump rings. First, pull a jump ring open using pliers, then close it around the chain. Then, open another jump ring and hook it through the eye pin; thread it through the chain's jump ring and close it.

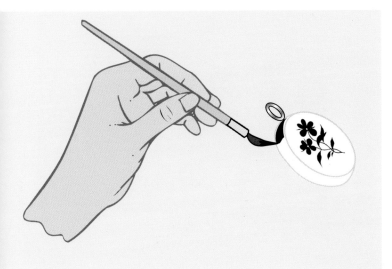

STEP 3

Paint the pendant and pin. Lightly sand the edges of the pendant and pin if necessary to smooth the surface. Glue the pin backing in place using permanent adhesive. Paint the edges and back of the pendant with silver paint. Finally, finish with a coat of varnish, if desired.

Variation:

Try using a solid black image on glitter or pearlescent clay for a bolder look. Follow the directions for the main project, but use black paint to highlight the edges of the clay. Use a jump ring to connect the key chain's eye pin to the key ring.

Tiled *Backsplash*

These nature-themed tiles make a serene and soothing accent to a room. Use them on walls or on furniture, such as a tabletop. The tiles can be directly applied to a surface or to a plank of wood to create an easy-to-handle inset. Or, border the plank with strips of painted wood as seen here, and use it as is. Rather than using cement grout, use polymer clay mixed with sand, which won't damage the tile surfaces. Finish with several coats of polymer clay gloss varnish for a glazed ceramic look.

MATERIALS

- *white polymer clay*

- *colored polymer clay for grouting*

- *sand*

- *rolling pin*

- *cookie sheet*

- *¹⁄₄" (5 mm) thick craft wood strips, at least 12" (30 cm) long*

- *Translucent Liquid Sculpey (TLS)*

- *sharp craft knife or tissue blade*

- *wood carving V-gouge*

- *wood carving flat chisel*

- *sponge applicator brush*

- *palette knife*

- *varnish*

- *fine sandpaper*

Starting *Out*

Wood carving tools work wonderfully with polymer clay and can be used to create a variety of effects. For this project, a flat chisel was used to smooth and even out the edges of the tiles quickly and easily. The art for these projects can be found on pages 294 and 295.

STEP 1

Prepare the artwork. Photocopy or print out the artwork to be used. Next, cut out the artwork, trimming as close to the images as possible. Make sure color copies are deep and rich. For ink jet printouts, use photo-quality paper and print the images on the setting suggested by the paper manufacturer. This is essential— printouts on regular paper will not transfer at all, but photo-quality paper yields an even better transfer than a color copy. (For more on preparing images, see the Tips & Tricks on page 13.)

STEP 2

Shape and bake the polymer clay. Knead a handful of clay until it is softened and very pliable. Place the 1/4" (5 mm) wood strips on the cookie sheet so that the rolling pin rests on them and there is ample space in between to roll out the clay. When the clay is 1/4" (5 mm) thick, place the transfer on top and gently trace the outline into the clay with a craft knife, toothpick, or similar tool. Then, remove the transfer, cut along the line, and remove the excess clay without disturbing the tile form. Next, brush a layer of liquid polymer transfer medium over the clay, then lay the transfer face down on the medium. Go over the surface lightly with the rolling pin once. Bake the tiles on the cookie sheet for no more than fifteen minutes at 275 degrees Fahrenheit (135 degrees Celsius). Wait for the tiles to cool before removing the paper.

To make several tiles at once, first cover the baking sheet with parchment paper. Prepare one tile, then carefully lift the parchment and set it aside. Make more tiles, rolling each on the baking sheet over parchment, and setting them aside as you go. Then, leaving them on the parchment, transfer all the tiles back to the baking sheet to bake together. Don't worry if the parchment overlaps the tiles because this won't cause any damage.

STEP 3

<u>Grout the tiles</u>. First, use a woodcarving gouge or similar tool to make shallow grooves in the back of each tile to aid adhesion. Next, lay the tiles down in the desired arrangement. Use sandpaper or a flat woodcarving chisel to trim the edges if necessary. To install, use strong, permanent glue. Next, knead a handful of polymer clay until soft and pliable to make grout. If desired, blend in sand for a more authentic look. The grout used here is a mixture of beige clay, translucent clay, and pale yellow sand. Smear the grout into the cracks between the tiles and smooth using a palette knife. Wipe away any excess on the tile surfaces. Then, bake again for 15 minutes at 275 degrees Fahrenheit (135 degrees Celsius).

Variation:

The advantage of using polymer clay to make tiles is the workability of the material and the speedy curing time. Virtually any image can be transferred to polymer clay with minimal color alteration. The coffee bean artwork on these tiles was made by colorizing a black-and-white photograph. See *Modifying Art by Hand and Computer* on pages 12–15 for more information.

Matisse *Kitchen Magnets*

Several coloring books are available from Dover Publications that are based on great paintings, spanning different periods and styles (See *Resources* on page 298 for ordering information). The magnets here are versions of Matisse paintings: *The Dream*; *Blue Nude I*; and *Nuit de Noël.* When coloring the images, keep in mind that bolder lines indicate black areas of the painting. The thinner guidelines indicate areas of the same color. Both colored artist's pencils and pastel pencils can be used. Look at art history books for inspiration to see the original colors of the paintings.

MATERIALS

- *white polymer clay*

- *colored pencils*

- *magnet tape*

- *¼" (5 mm) thick craft wood strips, at least 12" (30 cm) long*

- *rolling pin*

- *cookie sheet*

- *scissors*

- *sharp craft knife or tissue blade*

- *fine sandpaper*

Starting *Out*

For a rich, dark transfer, press firmly when coloring the photocopy to get lots of pigment on the paper. For a light wash of color, press lightly. The art for these projects can be found on page 296.

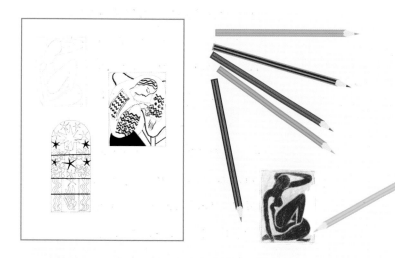

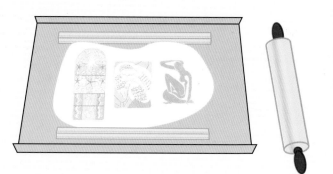

STEP 1

Prepare the artwork. Photocopy the artwork at the appropriate percentage on a black-and-white copier. The images supplied on page 296 are reversals of the original paintings. Next, color the images with pencils. Trim the artwork out, leaving an $^1/_8$" (3 mm) border of white around the image.

STEP 2

Shape and bake the polymer clay. Knead a small handful of clay for each magnet until it is softened and very pliable. Place the $^1/_4$" (5 mm) wood strips on the cookie sheet so that the rolling pin rests on them and there is ample space in between to roll out the clay. Roll the clay out until it is $^1/_4$" (5 mm) thick, then place the transfer face down and press it gently into the clay by going over it with the rolling pin once. Cut around the transfers using a craft knife or tissue blade. Rub the edges gently to smooth them out. Bake the magnets on the cookie sheet following the manufacturer's directions, generally fifteen minutes per $^1/_4$" (5 mm) of thickness at 275 degrees Fahrenheit (135 degrees Celsius). Once cool, remove the paper.

[**Tip:**]

If the transfer doesn't stick to the clay well, or if the corners begin peeling up, bake the magnets with a ceramic tile on top of them. The weight will keep the transfer in place evenly, and the tile won't be damaged by the oven's heat.

Variation:

These retro-inspired magnets make a fun, colorful addition to any refrigerator. Opaque heat transfer paper was used here for a crisp, unbroken image with virtually no color change. Simply bake it directly on raw clay, rather than ironing it on. And since the transfer is opaque, bright or dark-colored clay can be used without modifying the artwork. Use clay that matches the color of the fruit or vegetable for an easy bordered look, or just paint the edges of the finished magnets. Try using the same image at various sizes to make a whole "bunch" of tomatoes, peppers, mushrooms, or lemons. Be careful not to bake the magnets longer than recommended by the manufacturer. The ideal length of time, fifteen minutes, is sufficient to complete the transfer. Any longer may cause it to wrinkle unattractively.

STEP 3

Apply the magnet backing. Cut off an inch or two (3 cm–5 cm) of the magnet tape, remove the paper backing, and adhere it to one of the magnets. Repeat for each magnet, and add additional magnetic strips if necessary for larger magnets. Apply one or two coats of varnish to seal the magnets, if desired.

Suncatcher *Mobile*

These suncatchers are made of translucent polymer clay, which glows beautifully when bathed in light. The key to maximizing translucency, without sacrificing durability, is to roll the clay out to ¹/8" (3 mm) thick. Choose artwork that is brightly colored, with minimal, if any, white areas. For a striking display, make several mobiles of various lengths and stagger along a sunny window. For temporary hanging, use clear suction cups. For a more permanent solution, try screwing eye hooks into the top of the window frame.

MATERIALS

- *translucent polymer clay*

- *rolling pin*

- *cookie sheet*

- *¹/8" (3 mm) thick craft wood strips, at least 12" (30 cm) long*

- *translucent liquid polymer transfer medium*

- *embroidery floss or thread*

- *acrylic paint*

- *varnish*

- *fine sandpaper*

- *sharp craft knife or tissue blade*

- *eye pin*

- *small round brush*

- *sponge applicator brush*

Starting *Out*

Be sure there are no air bubbles caught between the clay and the paper transfer. Wait for the transfer medium to soak into and darken the paper, which should reveal any areas that aren't making contact. The art for these projects can be found on page 297.

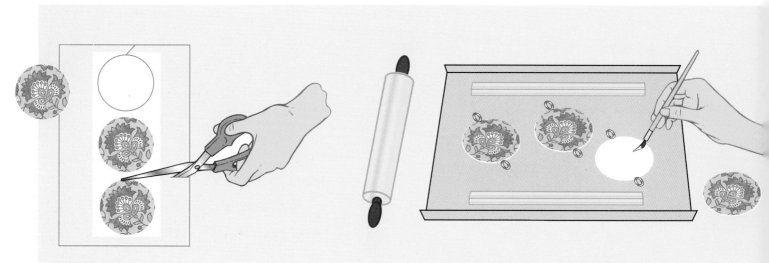

STEP 1

Prepare the artwork. Photocopy or print out the artwork to be used. Next, cut out the artwork, trimming as close to the images as possible. Make sure color copies are deep and rich. For ink jet printouts, use photo-quality paper and print the images on the setting suggested by the paper manufacturer. This is essential—printouts on regular paper will not transfer at all, but photo-quality paper yields an even better transfer than a color copy.

STEP 2

Shape and bake the polymer clay. Knead a small handful of clay until it is softened and very pliable. Place the 1/8" (3 mm) wood strips on the cookie sheet so that the rolling pin rests on them and there is ample space in between to roll out the clay. When the clay is 1/8" (3 mm) thick, place the transfer on top and gently trace the outline into the clay with a craft knife, toothpick, or similar tool. Then, remove the transfer, cut along the line, and remove the excess clay without disturbing the suncatcher form. Insert eye pins that have been trimmed to about 1/4" (5 mm) in length at the top and bottom of each suncatcher. Next, brush a layer of liquid polymer transfer medium over the clay, then lay the transfer face down on the medium. Go over the surface lightly with the rolling pin once. Bake the clay on the cookie sheet following the manufacturer's directions for baking the transfer medium. Bake no more than fifteen minutes at 300 degrees Fahrenheit (150 degrees Celsius).

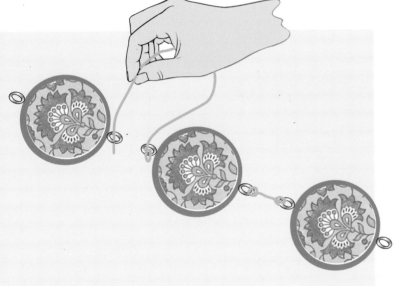

STEP 3

Assemble the mobile. Once the suncatchers are cooled, peel the paper off to reveal the transfer. Then, paint the edges, if desired. Apply a coat of varnish to each suncatcher. String them together using lengths of embroidery floss or invisible nylon thread.

Variation:

Suncatchers can be made in any shape. Experiment with different finishes for the edges as well. Silver foil tape, used by stained glass artisans as a base for leading, covers the edges of these suncatchers. Also try gilding foil, ribbon, or paper.

Handcoloring
Photos

THE BASICS

Sanford's Prismacolor pencils were used in many of the demonstrations in this book. Prismacolor pencils are made in a variety of colors and have a soft lead that will not scratch the surface (emulsion) of the print. Most colored pencils, however, will work just fine for hand coloring.

Colored pencils are great for hand coloring photographs because they're not intimidating like a paintbrush can be—you don't need special skills to use them. We've all been using pencils for most of our lives, and you probably even have some colored pencils around the house. A wonderful part of working with colored pencils is that

mistakes can be removed with a cotton swab moistened with a very small amount of water, making this a very forgiving medium for hand coloring.

In some of the demonstrations, a solution of turpentine and vegetable oil is used as a solvent for the colored pencils. The solvent is used to create a wash of color so the pencil strokes are not apparent on the print. Applied with a cotton swab, the oil allows the color to move around, creating the wash, and the turpentine cuts the oil slick on the print. This technique produces a transparent color that doesn't obscure the photograph; the color appears to be a part of the image rather than sitting on the surface of the print. Turpentine-and-oil solution can also be used to remove excess color. But be careful not to use too much solution. A very little goes a long way, as is explained in this book.

When learning to hand color, be sure to make multiple prints of the image being hand colored. This way you can experiment and compare the effects of different procedures and mediums. Keep records of each step so you can duplicate results you like.

LEMON YELLOW

FLESH

MAGENTA

CYAN

GREEN

ORANGE

△ Colored pencils are ideal for hand coloring because they don't require special skills to use them. And even just a handful of colors, such as the ones shown here, can produce vivid results.

Materials

Other than the photographic prints, you probably already have many of the materials required for hand coloring. Colored pencils are essential. Either use what you already have, or buy a small basic set of pencils. The basic set will include the colors needed to get started and can be mixed to create other colors. Besides, specific colors can always be bought individually at a later date. You may also want to buy Sanford's Blender Pencil. It's useful for keeping two side-by-side colors from overlapping to create a third color. It's also helpful in cleaning up areas of unwanted color, and it can be used to make the transition from one color to another smooth.

Other necessary supplies include: a tray; cotton swabs; cotton balls; toothpicks; transparent tape; a pencil sharpener; tongs; a small container for water; matte spray; vegetable oil; odorless turpentine (or a turpentine substitute); and a small glass bottle, preferably with a narrow neck and a top (don't use rubber lids—the turpentine in the turpentine-and-oil solution will dissolve the rubber). Optional are a small glass or heavy plastic measuring cup, sepia toner, and nylon or soft, lint-free gloves.

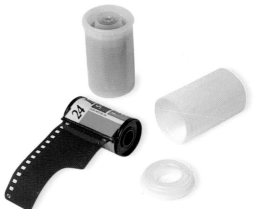

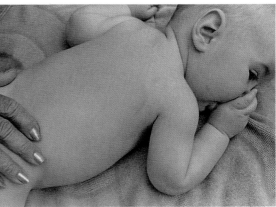

◁ 100-speed film

△ 400-speed film

△ High-speed infrared film

Film Types

The majority of photographs that are hand colored are taken with black-and-white film and are printed on black-and-white photographic paper. (A black-and-white print can be made from a color negative, but the results will be different.)

The photographs in this book were taken with three different film speeds: 100, 400, and high-speed infrared film. Which black-and-white film to use depends on the subject matter as well as the lighting conditions, the time of year, and whether you are shooting indoors or outdoors. When photographing outside in bright sunlight or even on bright overcast days in warmer weather, use a

slower film speed, like 100 or 125. These films have less grain and, in photographs of people, will render soft, smooth skin tones. For overcast, cloudier days, during the winter months, or when inside, use a faster film like 400, which is a bit grainy. In very low light situations without a flash, experiment with high-speed films, such as 1000 and above. Read the data sheet that comes with the film to become familiar with its characteristics.

Different kinds of film yield different effects or can evoke certain moods. For a romantic feel, try using a high-speed infrared film, which will produce a grainy look. Infrared film is a technical film that lends itself beautifully to hand coloring because it produces so many light/highlight tones.

◁ Photographs with a matte surface are ideal for hand coloring.

Print Surfaces

Photographic papers come in a variety of sizes, surfaces, types, and tones. Paper surface should be selected based on the materials being used to hand color. Matte surfaces, for instance, work the best regardless of the medium, but many materials won't adhere to a high-gloss surface. In fact, if you'll be using pencils, a flat matte surface is required. Oils can be used on a flat or semi-matte/pearl surface, and acrylics can be used on any surface. To make a print with a glossy or semi-matte/pearl surface suitable for hand coloring, spray it with matte spray to give it "tooth," or texture.

Print sizes vary. The easiest to hand color, and the size I recommend for beginners, is an 8" x 10" (20 cm x 25 cm) print. Anything smaller than this size will require more detailed work. Plus, larger prints are more expensive and take longer to color. After mastering hand coloring an 8" x 10" (20 cm x 25 cm) print, try working on a larger print. The results can be spectacular.

Photographic papers are either fiber-based or resin-coated (R/C). Photos printed on fiber-based paper are somewhat easier to hand color, and colored pencils appear slightly brighter on them. However, this paper is more expensive, and it takes longer to make a print on it than on resin-coated paper, which should be taken into account if you're doing the printing yourself. Keep track of the kind of paper you're using. Tonal qualities vary by manufacturer. Some papers are warmer or cooler toned, and some have a slight color cast. These characteristics will affect the results of hand coloring.

Shooting Images to Hand Color

Any subject matter and type of photograph can be hand colored. Landscapes, people, animals, architecture, interiors, vacation photos, or even scenes staged with props and costumes work well. The more you enjoy the subject matter and the photograph, the more fun you will have hand coloring the print.

Keep in mind, though, that the sharper the image, the better defined the potential hand-coloring areas will be. Areas that hand color the best are the light and highlight areas; color applied to dark areas of a print won't show up very well. Since the light/highlight areas are the most obvious areas to hand color, some hand colorists print their photos slightly lighter than usual.

Photographing with black-and-white film is different from using color film. All colors become a shade of gray, black, or white. If you're posing a shot, use props that are light in color, and have the subjects wear light-colored clothing. Since you are the artist, if you want the color of someone's sweater to be red, then have that person wear a pastel or very light-colored sweater and then color it the desired red after printing the photo. Learning how black-and-white film sees reality takes practice. Sometimes squinting or wearing dark sunglasses that are neutral in color helps simulate how the film reads colors.

Using Images of Your Own

Test existing black-and-white photographs you'd like to hand color to see if the surface of the prints will "take" the colored pencils. Take a bright-colored pencil and make two marks: one in the white border that surrounds the image and the other on a blank piece of paper. Compare the two marks to see if they look similar. If they do, then the print can be hand colored. If the pencil barely makes a mark on the print or comes off when rubbed, then the print surface is not suitable. (Remember, the mark can be erased with a small amount of water and a cotton swab.) In the latter case, use matte spray to give the print tooth (see "Print Surfaces"). One note on matte spray: If you overwork a sprayed print or use too much solution on it, the spray can come off in areas, and in those areas the color will not adhere.

When working with snapshots or vintage photographs, you may not want to use the original print. Instead, go to a lab and have either a copy negative or computer-generated negative made. Then have a black-and-white print made from that on matte-surface paper. You may have to go to a professional lab for this because most color labs print black-and-white film on color paper, and the tones and the surfaces will not be good for hand coloring.

Color prints are also an option. Color negatives can be printed on black-and-white paper, but the prints will need to be sprayed first if they are not printed on matte-surface paper.

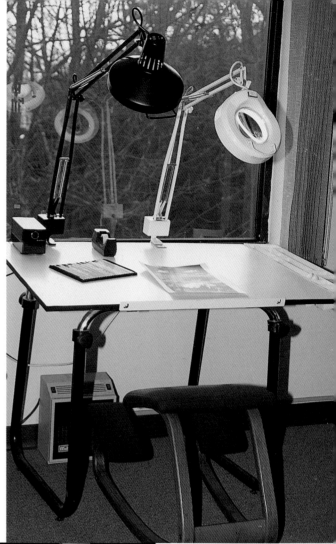

▷ Look for a smooth work surface, such as a drafting table or a regular table covered with a piece of acrylic or smooth mat board.

Work Area

Start with a smooth work surface. If it isn't smooth, the print will pick up its texture when it is hand colored, just as if it were a rubbing of the table. If you like to work at an angle, try a drafting table or a portable drafting table that can be placed on an existing tabletop. Drafting tables, which are adjustable, are available at most office-supply stores. To work on a flat surface, use a piece of acrylic or smooth mat board on a regular table.

Some of the materials used to hand color are toxic, so if you're working in your kitchen, be sure to keep your work area separate from food-preparation areas. Ventilation is also something to keep in mind. When using turpentine (in the turpentine-and-oil solution), it's a good idea to use an air purifier or keep a window open. When working outside,

avoid bright sunlight because the heat from the sun could curl the prints and make your pencil tips more apt to break.

Good lighting is essential in a work area. Natural light works well, as do lights that have both a fluorescent tube and a tungsten bulb. These lights give a natural, balanced light and are very bright. If working outside, choose a shady area.

◁ *Joanne, Kelly, Barton, and Stephanie*
by Laurie Klein
This photograph was over-matted with a
French mat. Some of the colors used in the
photo were also applied to the French mat.

the photo was printed on matte or semi-matte paper. Also, the small amount of residual oil from the solution or the waxy residue that colored pencils sometimes leave will not be visible.

Double mat your print, or at least place a mat over it to avoid contact with the glass. If the glass from the frame is flush against the print, the hand coloring will be transferred from the print to the glass. Using an over mat or double mat makes the piece look very professional.

I don't recommend dry mounting the print with a hot or cold press because the heat and rubbing necessary in this process can affect the hand coloring. Don't use an album that has acetate overlays. They can destroy photographic prints over a period of time. Your work of art is one of a kind and therefore irreplaceable. To make copies, either have a color laser copy made or have a lab make a color copy negative, from which a color print can be made.

Presentation

I do not recommend spraying a print after it has been toned and hand colored. The more chemicals (other than toners) that are applied to a print, the greater the chance it will deteriorate. Instead, try framing the photograph. This will protect it from moisture and dust, both of which could ruin the hand coloring that you have spent so much time creating.

Many people don't like the look of matte print paper because it has a dull, flat appearance. But once the print is behind glass, you won't be able to tell whether

▷ *Untitled*
by Laurie Klein
This photo is over-matted. The color of
the frame echoes that of the barn.

◁ This photo is framed very simply with
a beveled over-mat.

BASIC HOW-TO DEMONSTRATION

MIXING COLORS

A color wheel, which can be made or purchased, is helpful in understanding how to mix colors, such as making green out of blue and yellow. Harmonious colors are located next to one another on the color wheel. For example, red and orange are harmonious colors. Conversely, colors opposite each other on the wheel, such as red and green, are called complementary colors. They create a bold, dramatic feel, which is a much different mood. When complementary colors are mixed together, however, a muddy color results.

Colored pencils can be mixed directly on the print or in the white border area of the print. Using the blender pencil, blend the colors where they overlap, producing a third color. Another option is to use a separate piece of plain white photographic paper as a palette. Mix colors with the turpentine-and-oil solution and then transfer them to the print using a cotton swab.

CHOOSING COLORS

Choosing colors can be the hardest and yet most enjoyable part of the hand-coloring process. There are so many approaches. A photo can be colored realistically, interpreted with colors, or made to look surrealistic by using colors that are far from realistic and that allow the imagination to soar. Adding color to a black-and-white photograph establishes a mood or feeling. Always look at the image and get a sense of what you'd like to communicate. Hand coloring takes an image one step further, and the colors directly affect the message. If the goal is to make the print bold and graphic, for example, use vibrant colors.

It's important to maintain your colored pencils. Sharpen the end of the pencil that doesn't bear the name or number of the color so you'll know which one it is when you need to replace it. Also, make sure the tips aren't too sharp or long. To color large areas, use Prismacolor Art Stix.

Red, orange, and yellow are warm colors.

red + blue = purple

Greens and blues are cool colors.

red + yellow = orange

yellow + blue = green

Red and green are complementary colors.

Hand Coloring a Photo

Now it's time to jump in, take a pencil in hand, and actually color the photograph. But keep it simple. Sometimes the least amount of color creates the most interesting result. Remember that hand coloring an area changes the composition, so after choosing the first area to hand color, check the compositional balance. This may influence which area you choose to color next and how you color it.

Experiment with a solution that is equal parts vegetable oil and odorless turpentine. It's important to prepare this solution properly. If the print is too oily looking, there's too much oil in the solution; if all the color comes off, then there's too much turpentine (turpentine removes color). Store the solution in a small bottle with a lid. It will last for a long time. Don't leave the solution uncovered, though, because the turpentine will evaporate and the mixture will then be out of balance. Use as little solution as possible, and try not to use it too often. In small areas, for example, rubbing the color with a cotton swab is sufficient to smooth out the pencil strokes and remove waxy buildup.

△ This photo was chosen because there is no single focal point; each blade of grass has equal importance. Choose one blade of grass and color it in using the spring green pencil. (It will not be necessary to use solution.) Now the emphasis is on that one blade of grass.

△ Here, the whole image was colored with the same green pencil. Don't color each blade of grass individually; it will take
too long. Instead, create a color wash by using a small
amount of solution and a cotton ball. Solution was applied to
the left side of the photo, whereas the color on the right side
of the photo was not blended and the pencil marks are still
apparent. Leaving the marks unblended makes the color
appear to sit on top of the print instead of be a part of it.

No solution

▽ In this photograph, lighter, brighter colors were added to the grass in the foreground to give the image a three-dimensional look. Other greens were used, and pinks and oranges were blended with the spring green to create a warmer green. These variations of green make the image more interesting.

△ Color to capture the mood.

PEOPLE

Most of the photographs you already have are probably snapshots of family members and friends. You may have a lifetime of memories filed away—family vacations, weddings, birthdays, and anniversaries, or perhaps friends just having fun. Maybe you even have vintage photographs of ancestors. Have you ever wondered what else could be done with these photographs? Hand-colored photographs make wonderful, personal gifts. Hand coloring a photo gives the image a timeless quality and combines the realism of photography with the artistry of painting. With the popularity of memory albums and scrapbooks, many people are coloring vintage black-and-white and contemporary family photographs to preserve their family history. Chances are, most of your photographs are color prints or vintage black-and-white prints. Before you start to color, have "copy negatives" made, so that you can have multiple prints of the same photo and can preserve the original. Use the copies to experiment—try several different applications of color to achieve different results.

▷ Color for realism.

▷ Color photos to remember the moment.

Working with Photographs of People

When selecting a photograph to color, seek images with a lot of highlight areas (places that show white or a pale tone on the photograph). Images with lots of highlights work best for hand coloring. Selecting an image that is a close-up of someone's face allows you to color in skin tones or apply color like makeup. If the color is applied subtly, you can mimic the appearance of an "old-fash-ioned portrait." Color applied more boldly creates a contemporary effect.

Photographs of people in landscapes ("environmental" portraits) give you the opportunity to color both people and nature. Where you apply the color is a matter of artistic choice. Start with the part of the image that you feel is most important. It will be easiest to leave small details for last, after applying the main colors.

▷ Outdoor photos allow you to color both people and landscapes.

▷ Emphasize the foreground by adding color.

▷ Look for images with a lot of white areas.

Color is powerful. Even a little color added to a photo will change it entirely. Different colors create different moods: Reds, yellows, and oranges will make an image warm and inviting, while blues and greens produce a colder, fresher look. Use more than one shade of a color for a more natural effect. Blending and layering warm or cool colors will add dimension and realism.

If you want an area to stand out, try using a color that is opposite to the surrounding color—red against a green background, for example. Conversely, applying heavy layers of color will flatten the area somewhat, and put more emphasis on color than on the content of the image, making it less like a photograph and more like modern art.

△ The graphic qualities
and bold shapes of this
photograph make it very
appealing to hand color.

Hand Coloring a Contemporary Photo

GETTING STARTED

Try hand coloring photographs of people that are unique or abstract, as this image is. For example, a people photo without actual faces in it can be interesting and full of feeling. People often assume that when photographing someone, they should place the subject's head in the center of the viewfinder. But feel free to try something different. Play with the whole frame; move in close and place the subject in the corner of the frame. (See "The Basics" on page 109 for more on shooting images to hand color.)

MATERIALS

- black-and-white print on matte-surface paper
- colored pencils: flesh, blush, scarlet lake, true blue, olive green, metallic copper, imperial violet, green bice, orange, apple green, lemon yellow, violet blue
- cotton balls
- cotton swabs
- turpentine-and-oil solution
- Art Stix

FLESH   IMPERIAL VIOLET

BLUSH   GREEN BICE

SCARLET LAKE   ORANGE

TRUE BLUE   APPLE GREEN

OLIVE GREEN   LEMON YELLOW

METALLIC COPPER   VIOLET BLUE

△ **1**

Using the flesh pencil, color both babies' legs. Rub with a cotton swab to smooth in color (solution won't be necessary). Using the blush pencil, color the soles of the babies' feet, once again using the cotton swab to smooth the color in. Now use the flesh pencil again, moving from the legs to the soles of the feet, so it is not apparent where one color ends and the other begins. This is called "feathering."

Color the outfit on the baby in the upper-right section with the scarlet lake pencil. Use a cotton swab and a small amount of solution to smooth in the color so that no pencil marks are visible. Using the true-blue pencil, color the outfit on the baby in the lower-left section. Smooth the color in with a cotton swab and a small amount of solution, just as with the previous baby. Use a dry cotton swab on both outfits to remove any residual color or solution. To make the outfits deeper in color, apply a second coat. Use a dry cotton swab to smooth in the color.

TIP

○ Try using an olive-green
   Prismacolor Art Stix for the
   grass. Art Stix are terrific
   for coloring large areas.

◁ 3

Using the olive-green pencil, color the grass area. In the areas around the babies' bodies and clothing, use a small amount of solution on a cotton swab to smooth in the color. For the larger areas, use a cotton ball with a small amount of solution to smooth in the color. Color the blades of grass in front of the babies' feet with a sharpened olive-green pencil.

▷ 4

Use the orange, imperial violet, metallic copper, and green bice pencils on the grass to give it more depth. Select a few different blades of grass and color them individually for a more natural look. Smooth the color in with a cotton swab.

VARIATION

Complementary colors are perfect for making a statement.

1. Don't add any color to the babies' feet. Use the scarlet lake pencil for the grass to create a surrealistic effect. Use turpentine-and-oil solution on a cotton swab to smooth in the color.
2. With the apple-green pencil, color a few select blades of grass. Blend with a cotton swab. The red (scarlet lake) and green, which are complementary colors, add up to a bold statement.
3. Color the outfit on the baby in the upper-right section using the lemon-yellow pencil. Apply a small amount of solution to a cotton swab and smooth in the color. Using the violet blue pencil, color the outfit of the baby in the lower-left section. Use a small amount of solution on a swab for blending.

△ This image has a great deal of
mood, especially since the bride
and flower girl are looking at
one another and not directly into
the camera.

◁ The way the gray stonework and
stairs contrast with the pale
tones of the garments and flowers
makes this a wonderful image to
hand color.

Creating a Romantic Atmosphere

GETTING STARTED

This photograph was chosen because it is a candid depiction of the bride, ring bearer, and flower girl. They are the main subjects in the photograph, but the flowers and greenery can have as much emphasis if hand colored. Hand coloring them also strengthens the balance of the composition, echoing the triangular shape made by the bride and the children.

MATERIALS

- black-and-white print on matte-surface paper
- colored pencils: deco pink, olive green, lavender, sand, pink, salmon pink, brite purple, orange, lemon yellow, grayed lavender, true green, light peach/flesh, blush, true blue, raw umber, clay rose, terra-cotta, nonphoto blue
- cotton balls
- toothpicks
- cotton swabs
- turpentine-and-oil solution
- blender pencil
- sepia toner

DECO PINK

GRAYED LAVENDER

OLIVE GREEN

TRUE GREEN

LAVENDER

LIGHT PEACH/FLESH

SAND

BLUSH

PINK

TRUE BLUE

SALMON PINK

RAW UMBER

BRITE PURPLE

CLAY ROSE

ORANGE

TERRA-COTTA

LEMON YELLOW

NONPHOTO BLUE

△ 1

Sepia-tone the print. (See "Advanced Techniques" on page 144.) Use the deco pink pencil to color the top and bottom of the bride's dress, applying very small amounts of solution to smooth in the color. Use the same pencil for the flower girl's hairpiece. Smooth the color in with a fresh cotton swab.

△ **2**

Color the foliage with the olive-green pencil. Use a small amount of solution to smooth in the color.

TIPS

○ To remove a color, use a tooth-pick with a very small amount of water on it. Wait a few minutes for the water to dry (the color won't adhere if the print is wet), and then reapply color.

○ To soften the line where two colors meet, try using the blender pencil.

▷ **3**

Using the lavender pencil, color the satin wrap on the stems of the bouquet. Use the sand pencil to color the large flower. Also use the sand pencil on select smaller flowers to balance the large flower. Use the pink, salmon pink, and brite purple pencils to color the remaining flowers. A little solution may be necessary for blending. Use a toothpick wrapped tightly in cotton with some solution for blending small areas, or try using the blender pencil instead. Use the olive-green pencil to color the darker areas around and within the flowers to add depth.

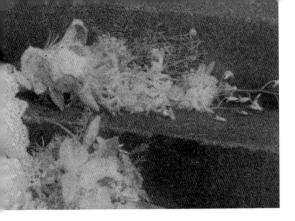

◁ **4**

Hand coloring is a way to strengthen or even alter the composition of a photo. Use the sand, lemon yellow, salmon pink, pink, and grayed lavender for the flowers on the steps. Try layering colors, such as yellow over pink. Use the true green for some of the foliage in the bouquets and olive green to add depth between and within the flowers. These colors, which are from a slightly different palette than those used in the bride's bouquet, draw the viewer's attention up and around the steps.

VARIATION

Bold hues can heighten the sense of romance.

1. Use the light peach/flesh pencil to color all skin areas. Then, using a very small amount of solution on a toothpick wrapped in a cotton ball, smooth in the color.

2. Moving the pink pencil in a circular motion, color the cheek areas. Blend with a fresh cotton swab so the color doesn't appear to be on top of the skin tone, but rather looks like it's a part of it. Use a sharpened blush pencil to color in the lips.

3. The true-blue pencil was used on the boy's eyes. The girl's hair was colored with streaks of lemon yellow in the lighter areas and raw umber in the darker strands of hair.

4. Use the lemon yellow to lightly color the lighter strands of the boy's hair to highlight and add luster, creating depth and balancing his hair with the girl's.

5. Color the bride's earrings with the sand pencil. Use the clay-rose pencil and solution to color the background stone and steps.

6. Use the olive-green pencil and solution for all the foliage in the lower left and upper right. The terra-cotta pencil can be used on a few leaves; blend with a dry cotton swab for depth.

7. On the boy's and girl's outfits, use the nonphoto blue. Experiment with different colors in the flowers, using bold complementary colors.

△ Begin with a copy of your favorite black-and-white portrait.

▷ Colored pencils make soft, muted hues, so prints with lots of light tones work best. Details in the dress give you areas in which to be creative and experiment with color.

Hand Coloring a Vintage Photograph

GETTING STARTED

Start by choosing a black-and-white print with a matte surface. Any image you have on hand can be used. If all your photographs are in color, have a black-and-white copy negative made and then printed on matte-surface paper. Most photo labs can easily make one for you. Likewise, if you have selected a vintage black-and-white photograph, it is a good idea to have a copy negative and print made. Then you can work on the re-print rather than coloring the original. Sepia-toning your prints will give them an antique look and can make even the most recent photographs seem vintage. When choosing a photograph to color, remember that lighter tones will show colors best.

MATERIALS

- black-and-white print on matte-surface paper
- colored pencils: flesh, pink, blush, scarlet lake, true blue, lemon yellow, canary yellow, mineral orange, crimson red, lavender, marine green, white, vermilion red, green bice
- cotton balls
- toothpicks
- cotton swabs
- turpentine-and-oil solution
- sepia toner

FLESH   MINERAL ORANGE

PINK   CRIMSON RED

BLUSH   LAVENDER

SCARLET LAKE   MARINE GREEN

TRUE BLUE   VERMILION RED

LEMON YELLOW   GREEN BICE

CANARY YELLOW

▷ 1

First, sepia-tone the print. (See "Advanced Techniques" on page 144.) Then, choose the most important areas and color these first. For this sepia-toned print, a flesh-colored pencil was used for the skin. Work with a back-and-forth motion to fill the whole area with color, then gently rub in the color with a cotton swab. For small areas, use part of a cotton ball wrapped around a toothpick.

△ **2**

A sharpened scarlet lake pencil adds brilliant color to the lips. A sharp-pointed true-blue pencil accents the eyes. Create contour in the cheek area with the pink pencil, or, if you want a look that is more subtle, you can use the blush pencil. To add accents to the hair, try using the lemon-yellow pencil in the lighter areas. Wipe away any excess pencil wax with a cotton swab.

▽ **3**

Using light, even strokes, color the clothing next. Dab a tiny amount of solution on the print with a cotton swab. With a different cotton swab, use a circular motion to rub in the color; aim for a uniform, transparent wash.

TIPS

○ For more vibrant skin tones, mix crimson red and white instead of using the flesh pencil.

○ Erase mistakes with cotton swabs and small amounts of water.

○ Make sure the entire area is filled with color before rubbing with the swab.

○ Go over areas twice to enhance color saturation. Use a new swab for each color.

○ If dark areas look shiny, swab them with a little water to dull them.

◁ 4

Contour the folds in the clothing with an accent color, such as mineral orange, to create depth. To finish, use crimson, lavender, and marine green pencils on details such as the garland of flowers. The same colors are also used on neckline to give the image harmony. True-blue pencil in the background and scarlet lake hues in the rug complete this hand-colored photograph.

VARIATION

A different palette creates
a completely different mood.

1. Color skin tones as in step one.
2. Use vermilion red to color the hair, then accent with canary yellow in the highlight areas for depth.
3. True blue and green bice create heightened contrast in the clothing. Green in the folds of the dress brings the color up into the bodice for continuity.
4. Use vermilion red on accents, such as the flower trim here.
5. Shade crimson on the background and blend smooth with a little solution on a cotton ball. On the areas close to the body, you may need to use a swab for better control. Canary yellow works well for small highlight areas in the background.

△ Hand coloring brings
out the textures.

▷ This image had a great
deal of mood even
before it was hand
colored.

Hand Coloring for Realism

GETTING STARTED

The texture of the tree trunk in this photograph made it an interesting selection to hand color. Different colors were used to create even more texture. Hand coloring everything except the young boy distinguishes him from the background, which also makes the photo look more three-dimensional.

MATERIALS

- black-and-white print on matte-surface paper
- colored pencils: spring green, terra-cotta, sienna brown, pink, canary yellow, poppy red, metallic copper, carmine red, Copenhagen blue, flesh, crimson red, peacock blue, sand, blush
- cotton swabs
- turpentine-and-oil solution

SPRING GREEN

CARMINE RED

TERRA-COTTA

COPENHAGEN BLUE

SIENNA BROWN

FLESH

PINK

CRIMSON RED

CANARY YELLOW

PEACOCK BLUE

POPPY RED

SAND

METALLIC COPPER

BLUSH

▷ 1

Apply an even wash of spring green on the grass. To create the wash, apply the color and then smooth it in with a cotton swab soaked in a small amount of solution. Take your time when smoothing in the color so that it will be consistent throughout the grass. Continue to use fresh cotton swabs until you get an even wash. To clean areas where the color has bled, use a fresh cotton swab and a small amount of water.

▷ **2**

Color the larger tree using the terra-cotta pencil. Using a small amount of solution on a cotton swab, smooth in the color. Use the sienna brown for the trees in the background. Blend with a small amount of solution.

◁ **3**

To create more depth, use the pink pencil to color random areas of the grass. The mixture of the coolness of the green in the grass and the warmth of the pink adds depth. Smooth in the color with a cotton swab.

TIP

○ Use the sunlight in a photograph as a guide when choosing an image to hand color. In this photograph, for example, it appears to be late afternoon. The shadows are long and angular and create warm sunlight on the tree trunk for contours and depth.

◁ **4**

Use the canary yellow and poppy red pencils to color the lighter (highlighted) areas of the tree. (Tree bark is never just one color. Using other colors makes the trunk appear three-dimensional. Blend with a dry cotton swab.) Color the dirt area in the grass and the other shadow areas with the metallic copper pencil, using a small back-and-forth motion. This adds contrast (by making it darker) and warms up the area. Use a cotton swab to lightly rub the color in.

VARIATION

Experiment with bold colors on dyed or toned prints.

This photograph was dyed using tea. (See "Advanced Techniques" on page 144.) Stronger colors are necessary for prints that are heavily dyed or toned.

1. Use carmine red, a warm color, for the pants, adding crimson red in the darker folds to show the contours.
2. Color the sweatshirt with Copenhagen blue, a cool color. Use peacock blue in the folds.
3. Use the sand pencil for the highlights in the boy's hair. Flesh can be used on his face and hand, with blush added on his cheek.

PLACES

Photographs of landscapes and nature are wonderful to hand color. Black-and-white photographs of sunsets, for example, can be hand colored to create a romantic or serene feel. Photographs of clouds taken before or after a storm also can be the basis of a dramatic hand-colored image.

Another advantage of landscapes is that they lend themselves to a three-dimensional look. Use darker and more saturated colors in the foreground and lighter and less saturated ones for objects that appear farther away from the viewer. Coloring the sky area blue adds to the effect of distant objects receding. Choose a palette to create the desired mood.

Other possibilities include photographing pets outdoors. Then there are flowers and wild animals, although a macro setting or close-up attachment may be necessary to photograph flowers (many zoom lenses have macro settings as a feature). Try photographing your house and then hand coloring it and sending it as a postcard. Boats and interesting architecture are excellent subjects for hand coloring. Amusement parks, with their bright lights and action, are great to photograph and hand color. Experiment with slow and fast shutter speeds to capture the energy of the rides, then use vibrant colors to color the image. It's also fun to hand color photographs of still lifes arranged using fruit, flowers, and shells.

You may already have these types of photographs at home. Just remember that when picking out prints to hand color—or when actually photographing images to hand color—choose one with as many highlight areas as possible, since that is where color shows up best.

Hand color to add drama and depth to landscapes.

△ Use a mix of warm and cool colors to create a three-dimensional look.

Working with Photographs of Places

Many painters take a color photograph of a scene and then use it as a reference when painting. There's a lesson to be learned here. To hand color a photograph realistically, take two photographs of the same scene—one in black and white (to hand color) and one in color (as a reference).

When hand coloring with colored pencils, experiment to determine a palette that works well for you. Use a mix of warm and cool colors to create a three-dimensional look. Try hand coloring only select areas of the print for emphasis. Achieve a surreal effect by using colors in unexpected ways: Color the grass purple or add stars or even spaceships in the sky—it's up to your imagination!

▷ Although this picture was taken on a foggy day, which might have resulted in a dark print, the ice-covered pine needles came out pale enough to hand color because they reflected the available light.

There are several things to look out for when photographing nature. Something that in person looks like the perfect subject for hand coloring may not be so ideal in a black-and-white photograph. Pine trees, for example, often appear too dark to hand color. Wait until the sun is shining directly on them before taking the photograph and the trees will appear lighter in the print. The same goes for buildings that are in shadow: They will appear darker in black and white.

As for hand coloring nature shots, since so much in nature is green, try using a palette with more than one type of green. Use yellow-green and blue-green, and create your own green by adding pink, orange, or lavender to an existing green hue.

△ The depth of the scene, the different textures in the grass, and the deer make this
photograph a good candidate for hand
coloring. An image with a distinct foreground, middle ground, and background
offers the opportunity to enhance the illusion of depth.

Hand Coloring an Animal in a Landscape

GETTING STARTED

Photographs of animals are wonderful to hand color because of all the different textures in fur and feathers. For the best results, choose an image of an animal that is light to medium in color. This image has been sepia-toned (see "Advanced Techniques" on page 144.) to restore the warmth of the animals' coats as well as that of the landscape. Many different colors have been used to bring out the details in this photograph. Compare the photograph that was not hand colored to the finished one to observe the difference in depth. In the hand-colored photo, the ocean appears even farther away because of the cool blue used on it; the colors in the middle ground gradually increase in saturation toward the foreground of the scene to add dimension.

MATERIALS

- black-and-white print on matte-surface paper
- colored pencils: dark brown, terra-cotta, lemon yellow, sienna brown, light yellow-green, light peach, deco peach, salmon, light violet, deco blue, light flesh, nonphoto blue, sand, clay rose, olive green, dark green, pink, purple, orange
- cotton balls
- toothpicks
- cotton swabs
- turpentine-and-oil solution
- sepia toner

DARK BROWN

DECO BLUE

TERRA-COTTA

LIGHT FLESH

LEMON YELLOW

NONPHOTO BLUE

SIENNA BROWN

SAND

LIGHT YELLOW-GREEN

CLAY ROSE

LIGHT PEACH

OLIVE GREEN

DECO PEACH

DARK GREEN

SALMON

PINK

LIGHT VIOLET

PURPLE

ORANGE

▷ **1**

Sepia-tone the print, then use dark brown to color the deer. The dark-brown pencil is relatively soft, so solution is not needed. After applying color to both deer, use a cotton swab to gently rub the pigment in.

TIP

○ Moisten a cotton swab with water and wipe the foam areas of the ocean to pull off some of the blue and brighten the look of the water.

△ 2

Use the nonphoto blue pencil to fill in the water. Smooth the color in gently with a small amount of solution. Use the sand and clay-rose pencils for the beach and sand dunes. (See "Color Mixing" on page 114.) Use olive green to fill in the grass, and smooth the color in with a cotton swab. Blend the entire area with a cotton ball, but use a cotton swab at the border where the colors meet.

▷ 3

Add details and texture to the deer's coats with lemon-yellow, sienna brown, and terra-cotta pencils. Use the lemon yellow to add highlights, and use the two browns for the darker areas in the coat and around the deer's face.

◁ **4**

Using a single color for an entire area tends to flatten the image. To avoid this in the grass area, add other colors either in sections, on individual blades of grass, or on random leaves. To add visual interest, use colors like pink, purple, and orange in the grass. It is important to work each color throughout the composition to help balance and unify the image as a whole.

VARIATION

Color everything but the focal point to emphasize its importance.

1. For the grass, first apply yellow-green pencil and then use light peach and deco peach for accents.
2. Color the ocean with nonphoto blue, and use blue deco on the dark parts of the waves.
3. Use a blend of the light flesh and sand pencils on the beach and the dunes.
4. Leave the deer uncolored.

△ This photo is a great example of creating a color wash using colored pencils in order to cover large expanses of a photograph.

▷ This image already has many textures. Hand coloring, however, gives it a lot of depth, too.

Hand Coloring Nature

GETTING STARTED

Coloring each individual leaf in the foliage area of a picture such as this one would be very time-consuming. Instead, color was added and the turpentine-and-oil solution was used to create a wash. Other colors were then used on individual leaves to create depth. A mix of dark and bright colors was used in the foreground. The blue in the sky area makes it recede into the distance. In the hilly area beneath the sky, a lighter green was used. The light green in this area produces a hazy quality, which is exactly what you see when viewing hills from a distance.

MATERIALS

- black-and-white print on matte-surface paper
- colored pencils: flesh, raw umber, terra-cotta, chartreuse, nonphoto blue, olive green, spring green, green bice, parma violet, peacock blue, dark brown, dark green, true blue
- cotton balls
- toothpicks
- cotton swabs
- turpentine-and-oil solution
- blender pencil

 FLESH   GREEN BICE

 RAW UMBER   PARMA VIOLET

 TERRA-COTTA   PEACOCK BLUE

 CHARTREUSE   DARK BROWN

 NONPHOTO BLUE   DARK GREEN

OLIVE GREEN   TRUE BLUE

SPRING GREEN

△ 1

Color the pathway using the flesh pencil. Use a small amount of solution to smooth in the color, and use a cotton swab to pick up any excess. Use the dark-brown pencil to color the shadows created by the trees and fence in the pathway. This creates a realistic look of contrast and depth. Using a toothpick wrapped in cotton, smooth in the color so the pencil strokes are not apparent.

◁ 2

Apply a small amount of solution in the sky area, and then add nonphoto blue. Use a cotton swab to smooth in the color. (Here, the order of applying color and then solution was switched. See which way is better for you.) Don't worry if you get some blue in the leaves. Either use the blender pencil to tone down the blue in the leaves or try applying olive green to the leaves. Color the mountains using the chartreuse pencil. Using a toothpick wrapped in cotton, blend the color with solution. The color will be fairly light. There aren't many dark areas in the mountains, but the lighter wash will suggest depth.

TIP

○ Where one color meets another, a third color will be formed. To make this a smooth transition, use the blender pencil.

▷ 3

Create a color wash for the foliage instead of coloring each individual leaf. Color in one area of bushes or trees, and use a small amount of solution on a cotton swab to create an overall smoothness. Green bice was used on the bush in the foreground. The bush behind it was colored with a mixture of the dark-green and true-blue pencils. More than one layer may be necessary to create saturated, intense colors. By using the same two-color mix for the bush on the left (not shown here) a balance is created. A wash of the olive-green pencil was used in the remaining foliage. The chartreuse pencil was used to accentuate a few random leaves to create depth in the bush. The olive-green pencil was used in the remaining foliage.

◁ **4**

Use the raw umber pencil to color the railing. To eliminate the pencil strokes, wrap a tiny bit of cotton dipped in a very small amount of solution on a toothpick. You can also choose not to blend it, since pencil strokes add texture. Using the terra-cotta pencil, color the trees. Use heavier layering in the tree trunks. Color the limb areas with the same pencil. There may still be a slight residual of solution on the print, so if blending is necessary, use a cotton swab. Use the spring green pencil for the foreground foliage areas. Use a cotton swab and a small amount of solution to create a wash.

VARIATION

Selective hand coloring adds emphasis to key areas of a photograph.

1. Use the parma violet pencil to color the pathway, and blend the color with a small amount of solution.
2. Using the peacock blue pencil, color the shadows of the trees on the path. Using warm and cool tones in conjunction with dark tones over lighter tones creates contrast and depth.
3. Using the peacock blue, color the railing. To add texture, let the pencil strokes remain visible.

△ This photo was chosen because every area has equal importance.

▷ Flowers are one of the best subjects to hand color. They contain many details, which makes them great for learning and practicing different techniques.

Hand Coloring Flowers

GETTING STARTED

With any photograph, it is natural for the viewer's eye to be drawn to the lightest area of the print. Because the lightest area of this print is right on the edge, the viewer's gaze drifts off the page. To prevent this from happening and to create a tighter composition, add color to any edges that appear to be too light. Use the turpentine-and-oil solution as little as possible so the color does not become too thin. Layer the colors to make them appear more saturated and bolder.

MATERIALS

- black-and-white print on matte-surface paper
- colored pencils: salmon pink, scarlet lake, brite violet, Spanish orange, pink, grape, vermilion red, magenta, lemon yellow, deco peach, sand, metallic maroon, olive green, green bice, flesh
- cotton balls
- toothpicks
- cotton swabs
- turpentine-and-oil solution
- sepia toner

SALMON PINK   LEMON YELLOW

SCARLET LAKE   DECO PEACH

BRITE VIOLET   SAND

SPANISH ORANGE   METALLIC MAROON

PNK   OLIVE GREEN

GRAPE   GREEN BICE

VERMILION RED   FLESH

MAGENTA

▷ **1**

First, sepia-tone the photo. (See "Advanced Techniques" on page 160.) Then, choose which flower to hand color first, and use salmon pink to fill it in. Notice how the flower stands out against the uncolored background. Keep in mind that since salmon pink was used in such a large area of this print, it needs to be repeated in another area to balance the color composition. Watch how the color balance shifts as different colors are added to the remaining flowers.

◁ **2**

Color each flower with a base color.
The palette used for this image consists
mainly of pinks, peaches, and yellows.
This gives it a warm, harmonious look.
(See the section on choosing a palette
in "The Basics" on page 115.)

TIP

○ Select a palette in advance to
ensure the final image appears
unified in color.

▷ **3**

After filling in the flower with the
sand-colored pencil, use magenta in
the darker areas of the flower to add
depth and to tie in the colors in adja-
cent flowers.

◁ **4**

Using the olive-green pencil, color all the leaves. Then, use the green bice for the sprigs in front of various flowers.

VARIATION

Hand color selected areas of a toned image for a delicate look.

1. Using a sepia-toned print, color the rose with scarlet lake. Blend the color with a small amount of turpentine-and-oil solution.
2. Use olive green in the shadow areas of the rose for depth.
3. Use canary yellow in the highlight areas of the rose to add contour.
4. Color the sprigs, alternating canary yellow and green bice.
5. Color the bee with canary yellow to distinguish it from the flower.

△ The simplicity of this photograph makes it excellent
for hand coloring.

▷ A large sky area allows for the
application of blue, which
instantly creates a three-
dimensional look, since cool
colors always appear to recede.

Hand Coloring Architecture

GETTING STARTED

Photographing architecture of all kinds can be great fun. You can create a personal postcard, for example, using a photo of your home, boat, or car to send to friends or family. Just have a 4 x 6 (10 cm x 15 cm) or 5 x 7 (13 cm x 18 cm) black-and-white print made on matte paper from the negative, and then add some color. On the reverse side, create the look of a store-bought postcard by adding a dividing line down the middle and lines for the address with a fine-point permanent marker. Alternatively, you can buy a premade stamp at a craft store. Keep in mind that after the photograph goes through the mail, it will have been stamped by the post office and will probably look a little worn. These nuances are part of the beauty of postcard art.

MATERIALS

- black-and-white print on matte-surface paper
- colored pencils: true blue, vermilion red, magenta, grape, blue violet, terra-cotta, brite violet, metallic purple, sand, Tuscan red
- cotton balls
- toothpicks
- cotton swabs
- turpentine-and-oil solution
- fine-point permanent marker (optional)
- transparent tape (optional)

TRUE BLUE   TERRA-COTTA

VERMILION RED   BRITE VIOLET

MAGENTA   METALLIC PURPLE

GRAPE   SAND

BLUE VIOLET   TUSCAN RED

▷ **1**

Begin with the sky, using the true-blue pencil.

TIPS

- If color bleeds from one area into another, use the tip of a toothpick wrapped tightly in cotton and dampened with water to erase it or to clean up edges.

- Try applying the turpentine-and-oil solution before applying the color. Experiment and see which order works best for you.

- Use the solution on a cotton swab to blend in the color, and remove the pencil strokes with a cotton ball.

- To prevent the blue sky color from bleeding into other areas, mask these areas with transparent tape and remove the tape after the color has been smoothed in.

△ 2

Enhance the mood of an image by adding different colors to the sky area. Apply vermilion red to the horizon area and magenta directly above that. Feather the two colors together so it's not apparent where one begins and the other ends.

▷ 3

Above the magenta, use the grape pencil to darken the top of the sky. This creates the illusion of depth, since it separates the top of the lighthouse from the receding sky. To enhance this effect, add blue violet along the top of the print.

◁ **4**

Use terra-cotta for the top of the lighthouse. Notice how color applied in dark areas of a print has a subtle appearance.

VARIATION

Use varied colors for a dramatic sky.

1. Mask the lighthouse with tape.
2. Start at the bottom of the sky, using the sand-colored pencil.
3. Use the pink pencil above the area colored with sand, and blend the two colors where they meet with a little solution.
4. Use the brite violet pencil above the pink.
5. Finish the sky area with the metallic purple pencil.
6. Use the sand-colored pencil in the sky around the lighthouse to make it look like it's glowing.
7. Use a cotton ball to blend the whole sky area after all the colors have been applied.
8. Remove the tape from the lighthouse. Use Tuscan red for the upper section, leaving the very top uncolored, and remove any color from the window. Color the bottom section of the light-house canary yellow.

ADVANCED TECHNIQUES

With time, you'll get a feel for hand coloring and the effects it can produce. Then, consider trying another method to color black-and-white prints. Experiment with a variety of materials, such as oil paints, watercolors, or markers, to name a few. Make collages using your prints and other supplies from around the house. Some of these mediums will yield a heavier color treatment as well as texture (brushstrokes, finger marks, etc.).

Change the overall color of a print with household products such as grape juice, fabric dyes, coffee, tea, and food coloring. Anything that stains will work. Toners and nonorganic dyes are also an option. By making multiple prints of one image and trying different techniques on them, you can gain a better understanding of what effects each method produces. Keep records of what you do in case you want to re-create the result.

In this section, we'll look at toning, staining, dyeing, and painting with oils. Mix and match the different processes for different effects. By the time the artwork is finished, you may not even recognize it as having originated as a photograph!

▷ This photo was hand colored with both oils and colored pencils.

△ Blue toner was used to change the overall color of this image.

△ This photograph was toned and hand colored.

Working with Other Mediums

Choose a medium based on the desired effect. To change the overall color of the print, use toner, stains, or dyes, or create a wash using pencils or oils. For a textured look, try crayons or acrylics. To obscure the image, use an opaque medium such as air brushing, spray paint, acrylics, or oil pastels. You may want to mix mediums, adding bold, graphic lines of intense color with markers or metallic pens, or coloring with oil paints and using colored pencils for fine details. Try extending the image into the white borders of the print with pen and ink. Experiment with watercolors. Liquid or tube watercolors are more vibrant and work best on fiber-based paper, but mistakes are harder to remove, and the colors fade more rapidly.

▷ Colored pencils and oils added life to this photo.

△ Oils create a dreamy effect

▽ This photograph was toned
    brown and hand colored.

◁ This photograph
was simply toned.

Toners

What images tone best? Most toners are very vibrant in color, so strong, bold images work well. The most popular toner is sepia toner, which gives the image a timeless, antique look. Get a feel for the image first, and then you'll have a better idea of whether or not to tone the print and which toner to use.

Toner will affect different parts of a photo differently. White and highlight areas in the print will take on the exact color of the toner, but the color will look darker in mid-tone and shadow areas. It's a good idea to keep an extra, untoned print handy as a reference to gauge how heavily to tone the image. The effects of the toner also depend on the kind and brand of paper the photograph was printed on, whether the print is matte or semimatte, the toner type, how diluted the toner is, and how long the image is toned.

If you're interested in hand coloring part of the print after toning it, use rubber cement to mask that part of the print before toning. The color will be more vibrant that way. As a rule, when combining hand coloring and toning, always do the hand coloring last.

There are many different types and brands of toners on the market today, and photographic supply stores are the best place to find them. Some are in liquid form, some come as a powder. Some have one or two steps, some require many steps. Some toners are odorless, while others are not. Some are safe to use in the kitchen and around children, but the majority are not.

Toners can be reused if they are stored properly. Never use metal trays when working with toners, since these materials interact chemically. Use photographic trays because they are made of a heavy plastic and are meant soley for this purpose (unlike food trays).

Many toning processes include a bleach step. With these, make sure your images are 10–15% darker than they'd normally be printed. If you've never toned an image before, keep it simple: One toner per print. And remember: Always read the directions.

◁ This photograph was hand colored but not toned.

▷ Here's how it looks after it's been toned and hand colored.

Sepia Toning

GETTING STARTED

This photograph was chosen for sepia toning because the toner's brown color would lend the image warmth. It also would make the image appear timeless, giving a sense that this photograph could have been taken years ago. Toning and then hand coloring a print such as this one gives it a totally different feel, especially if it's hand colored with warm colors.

MATERIALS

- black-and-white print on matte-surface paper, printed slightly darker than normal
- colored pencils: nonphoto blue, spring green, hot pink, lilac, orange
- rubber cement
- five trays
- two pairs of tongs
- measuring cup
- sepia toner
- two dark plastic quart-size jugs for storing toner, one labeled "A," the other labeled "B"
- rubber gloves (optional)
- cotton swabs
- turpentine-and-oil solution

NONPHOTO BLUE

SPRING GREEN

HOT PINK

LILAC

ORANGE

▷ 1

Follow the instructions on the package for mixing, storing, and toning the toner in a well-ventilated area away from young children. (None of this, however, needs to be done in a darkroom or under subdued light.) The toner used in this example is a two-part toner, which can be mixed in advance and stored in dark jugs. Set up five trays next to each other. The first will be a pre-wash and holding tray for prints to be toned. In the second tray, pour enough of part "A" solution, which is the bleach step. Put one set of tongs in solution "A." Use only one set of tongs for each part—don't interchange them. The third tray is for washing the print in running water in between the chemical steps. In the fourth tray, pour solution "B," the brown toner, and add a pair of tongs. The last tray will be for rinsing the print in running water when you've finished toning.

△ **2**

Bleach until the shadows start to disappear. This print has been bleached for the full amount of time. The print will have a yellowish cast after being bleached.

▽ **3**

The browns from the toners will fill in the bleached areas, creating the sepia tones.

○ When bleaching a photograph, don't worry about losing the image; the image must bleach out. Bleaching is necessary so the brown tones can exist, which is why prints you plan to sepia tone should be darker than usual.

VARIATION

Use multiple toners to make key areas stand out.

1. Rubber cement was applied to the girl before the print was toned. This prevented bleach or toner from affecting that part of the print. As a result, the masked area has the original tones, which can be colored later or left as is. To use another toner color, mask the background with rubber cement, and tone just the girl. Start by using a cotton swab to apply rubber cement to the girl.

2. Tone as per instructions and allow the print to dry.

3. Rub off the rubber cement with your finger, and finish the print by hand coloring or retoning it.

△ This print was toned using copper/red toner, which is a liquid dye. It was left in the toner for only one minute.

△ This is how the photo looked before it was toned. It is useful to keep one untoned print as a guide. Wet the toned print before comparing it to the one you're working on, because prints are slightly darker when they are wet.

○ The most noticeable effects of toning will be in the shadow areas, but check the whites to see the true color of the toner.

Toning Photographs

GETTING STARTED

Produce different effects and moods by hand coloring toned and untoned prints. Placing a toned and an untoned print side-by-side is a good way to judge the effects of these experiments. When getting started in hand coloring and toning, make more than one print and compare the results.

MATERIALS

- black-and-white print on matte-surface paper
- measuring cup
- 3–4 trays
- 1–2 pairs of tongs
- 2–4 prints of the same image to experiment with
- blue toner
- red toner
- yellow toner

▽ This print was toned for ten minutes.

△ This print was toned
with blue toner for
ten minutes.

▷ This is how the photo
looked before it
was toned.

△ This print was toned
with yellow toner
for ten minutes.

▷ This is how the photo
looked before it
was toned.

Stains

The following pages contain staining demonstrations that are wonderful projects to do with children. The products used are readily available in many households. In fact, they're typically food items, like fruit punch and coffee, that are non-toxic and can be found in the kitchen. A few stains are mixed with hot water and need to be cooled to room temperature before using (hot liquid can ruin a print).

Since stains are usually less vibrant in color than toners and dyes, select images that are more subtle. The intensity of the colors can be altered, though, by varying the concentration of the stain and the length of time the print is stained. Keep records of the dilutions used in order to create the same results with a new batch of prints. (Note the dilutions on the back of the print with a waterproof marker.) Experiment with different household foods and see which results you like the best. Try different colored fruit punches, or create your own colors using food coloring. Try different types of teas. Regular tea, for example, creates a much deeper color stain than coffee does. Stains can be used over again. Store them in a labeled container in a cool place so they don't become moldy.

Set up a tray with water and soak the print for a minute before staining. This way, the emulsion is already saturated and will take the color as soon as it goes into the stain bath. After staining it, rinse the print in another tray of running water. (Change the water in this tray frequently.) Wash the print with room-temperature water for approximately five minutes. Take care when drying the print because stain can collect on the back or edges if dried improperly and can drip onto the image, resulting in uneven staining. Always hand color *after* dyeing or staining the prints.

△ This landscape photo
was stained with a
colored-pencil wash.

△ This photograph was
stained in wine for
ten minutes.

Staining Photographs

GETTING STARTED

Stains are usually less vibrant than toners and dyes. Select an image that contains a lot of highlights (lighter sections) and is subtle, like this photo of a boy looking out from a mass of leaves. This photo was stained with red wine at room temperature and then hand colored when it was completely dry. Some stains are made with hot water and therefore must be prepared in advance so they have time to cool to room temperature. When staining photos with food coloring or actual food or drinks (such as tea), it's okay to use kitchen trays or pans. Set up two trays: one with water, the other with stain. Use wooden or plastic tongs to keep from staining your hands.

MATERIALS

- black-and-white print on matte-surface paper
- colored pencils: crimson red, violet, scarlet lake, dark purple, chartreuse, hot pink, spring green, salmon pink, marine green, mulberry, lilac, orange
- red wine
- blue food coloring
- red punch
- coffee
- tea
- measuring cup
- glass or plastic trays large enough to accommodate prints
- cotton swabs
- turpentine-and-oil solution
- tongs

CRIMSON RED

SPRING GREEN

VIOLET

SALMON PINK

SCARLET LAKE

MARINE GREEN

DARK PURPLE

MULBERRY

CHARTREUSE

LILAC

HOT PINK

ORANGE

▷ 1

First, prepare the surface. Immerse the print in a tray filled with water. Leave it in for one minute. Remove it from the water and put it in a tray filled with staining bath. Use your judgment as to how long to keep it in the stain. Keep a record of the amount of time you soak the print in the stain as well as of the concentration of the stain. This way, you can keep track of how you obtained your favorite results.

◁ **2**

Boil four tea bags in approximately 20
ounces (600 ml) of water, then let the tea
steep until it cools to room temperature. This
print was stained for ten minutes. Rinse the
print for five minutes when done to remove
excess tea.

▽ **3**

Brew approximately 20 ounces (600 ml)
of coffee. Let it cool to room temperature.
This print was stained for ten minutes.
Rinse the print for five minutes when
done to remove excess coffee.

TIP

○ To dry prints, use a hair dryer
  at a low setting or hang the
  prints by a corner with a
  clothespin. Don't lay them flat
  to dry because excess color
  and water will collect and
  stain parts of the print darker
  than the rest.

◁ **4**

Mix 10 drops of blue food coloring with 20 ounces (600 ml) of room-temperature water. Allow the picture to soak for ten minutes. Rinse the print when done to remove excess food coloring.

VARIATION

Fruit punch produces an appealingly vibrant stain.

1. Immerse the print in water in the first tray.
2. Stain the print for ten minutes in fruit punch.
3. Rinse the print and hang it to dry.

◁ Rubber cement was applied to the stem of the branch before this print was dyed green for ten minutes.

Dyes

Dyes do not chemically react with a print; instead, they dye the base color of the print. Because of this, dyes are not as permanent as toners. If a print that has been dyed is exposed to strong sunlight for any length of time, it is likely to fade. Still, dyes are sometimes desirable because they often produce more brilliant colors than stains. Photographic or liquid dyes are available at art-supply and craft stores or at photo-supply stores.

Since most dyes are vibrant, choose a photograph that is compositionally strong and graphic—one with strong lines or shapes. Also look for action shots in which someone or something is moving, which you can capture by using a fast shutter speed (or use a slow shutter speed to blur the image). Combine colors to create a hue that suits the subject matter.

Dyeing a print is fairly simple. Combine the dye with water to create a dye bath. Immerse the print in the bath. You don't need to work in a darkroom, but it is still a good idea to keep dyes out of the kitchen area and to supervise young children. Be sure to read the directions since different manufacturer's dyes are handled differently.

Remember to keep records of your experiments with dyes so you can re-create results you like. Also, the general rule of thumb for hand coloring also applies to dyeing: The print should contain a lot of highlight areas. All hand coloring should be done after dyeing or staining a print.

▽ This photograph was dyed magenta for ten minutes.

△ Hand coloring with dyes works
for this photo because Ferris
wheels are associated with
bright colors.

Dyeing Photographs

GETTING STARTED

Dyes, which are usually very vibrant, are ideal to use on photographs of brightly colored subject matter, like a Ferris wheel. To add the illusion of movement in this photo, a slow shutter speed was used when the picture was taken. The photo was hand colored using a photographic flesh-colored dye.

MATERIALS

- black-and-white print on matte-surface paper
- lemon-yellow colored pencil
- plastic tray from a photo store
- tongs (wooden or plastic)
- measuring cup
- photographic dyes: flesh, magenta, magenta mixed with cyan, green, orange
- rubber cement
- small brush

LEMON YELLOW

FLESH

MAGENTA

CYAN

GREEN

ORANGE

△ 1

Prepare the surface by soaking the photograph in a tray of fresh water for at least one minute.

△ **2**

Prepare a tray with 20 ounces
(600 ml) of room-temperature
water. Add 10 drops of dye (in
this case, orange) to the water
and mix with the tongs. Make
sure the color is evenly dispersed.
After dyeing, wash the print in a
tray of fresh tap water at room
temperature for five minutes.
Hang the print to dry or use a
blow dryer at a low setting. This
print was dyed for eight minutes.

TIP

○ Make sure to use fresh water
and clean tongs when you go
from one colored dye to the
next. Staining or contamina-
tion can occur if you're not
careful.

▷ **3**

Try combining different colors to
create a new one. This color was
created by mixing 5 ounces (150 ml)
of magenta with 5 ounces of cyan in
20 ounces (600 ml) of water. The
print was dyed for ten minutes.

△ **4**

Mix 10 drops of green dye into 20 ounces (600 ml) of water. This print was dyed for eight minutes.

VARIATION

Contrasting colors bring out a picture's highlights.

1. Rubber cement was used as a mask to cover the lights on the Ferris wheel so they could be hand colored separately, adding color contrast to this image.
2. Pre-wash the print. Then, soak it in dye for eight minutes and allow it to dry.
3. Rub off the rubber cement with your finger, and hand color the lights using the lemon-yellow pencil.

▷ Some black-and-white postcards are perfect for hand coloring with oils.

Oils

Hand coloring with oils can produce a much different effect than using colored pencils. For starters, oil colors are slightly more intense and vibrant. Also, oils are noted for their permanence.

There are many different types of oil paints. Photographic oils are designed specifically for hand coloring prints. Oils can be used on a semimatte or matte paper, but if you plan to do detail work with colored pencils afterward, you'll need to work on matte paper. If you use artist's oil paints, try thinning the oils with transparentizing gel before using them. This will make them more transparent without affecting the intensity of the colors. Another option is to use extender, which can be added to oil paint to reduce color intensity.

Like pencils, oils are, for the most part, easy to remove (although some of the more vibrant colors do not come off so easily). Gently rub mistakes away with a cotton swab or cotton ball, or use the turpentine-and-oil solution or mineral spirits. If the print has white borders, protect them with transparent tape. This is also a fingerprint-free means of holding the photo down while you work on it.

▷ This postcard was
colored blue with
a wash of oil paint.

△ A good candidate for hand coloring, this photograph has strong elements in the foreground (the leaves) and a lot of depth.

First, prepare the print surface; otherwise, the colors may appear too strong. Using a cotton ball, apply a small amount of either mineral spirits or turpentine-and-oil solution directly to the print surface. (Resin-coated paper requires less solution than fiber-based.)

Using a palette, whether it is store-bought or just a plastic plate, is recommended. Place small amounts of oil paint directly on it and mix the colors with a toothpick. It's difficult to exactly re-create a mixed color, so be sure to mix more than you think you'll need.

Save any left-over color by putting the palette in a sealable plastic bag. Oils can take hours or days to dry anyway, depending on how thickly they have been applied, but the plastic bag is an extra measure to prevent them from drying. This way, you can come back to your print later to add more color.

Use cotton swabs to dab color directly
from the palette onto the print surface.
For large areas, use a cotton ball to
work the color in. For the smallest
areas, use a cotton swab or wrap a
toothpick with cotton and use it as a
paintbrush. For very fine details, try
using the end of a plain toothpick (but
don't press down hard with the toothpick—this can scratch the emulsion of
the print).

Layering colors will increase their intensity, but allow time for each layer to dry
before adding another or the paint
might crack.

▽ Oils were used to color the
large areas, such as the
grass, and colored pencils
were used to punch up the
small details, like the leaves.

◁ The beauty of hand coloring this image is its simplicity, yet a lot of detail work can be added to the tulips.

Adding Subtle Details
with Oils

GETTING STARTED

These tulips were photographed on top of a piece of black velvet to enhance the contrast. When working with large dark areas, like the background in this picture, wear nylon or cotton gloves, or place a piece of soft gauze between your hand and the surface of the print. This will prevent the oils from your hands from leaving marks in the dark sections. Start by adding color to the large areas of the flowers and end by doing the fine detail work. This is a great picture in which to mix mediums. Color the flowers and stems with oils, and add details in the flowers with either oils or pencils.

MATERIALS

- black-and-white print on matte-surface paper
- oils: yellow, yellow-green, warm red, cadmium orange, dioxazine purple, chartreuse, imperial violet
- cotton balls
- toothpicks
- cotton swabs
- turpentine-and-oil solution
- palette
- gloves

YELLOW

DIOXAZINE PURPLE

YELLOW-GREEN

CHARTREUSE

WARM RED

IMPERIAL VIOLET

CADMIUM ORANGE

▷ 1

Start with a semimatte or matte print. (Use a flat matte print if you plan to also use pencils.) Select your colors and place a small amount of each on a palette.

◁ **2**

Treat the surface of both tulips with solution. Apply imperial violet oil from the palette to the top tulip with a cotton swab. Use a circular motion to work the oil in so that it is smooth.

▷ **3**

Apply a small amount of warm red to a second tulip to complement the coolness of the imperial violet tulip, using the same circular motion with a cotton swab. Continue to use clean swabs until all the color is smoothed in.

▷ **4**

Use a toothpick wrapped tightly with cotton to apply a very small amount of yellow-green from the palette to the stems of the tulips. (It is not necessary to prepare the print surface of the stems for this step.) Have a few more toothpicks with cotton already made. Work back and forth until all the color is blended. If you accidentally get some of the color in the background area, erase it with a cotton swab moistened with a very small amount of water.

◁ 5

Flowers contain a lot of green. Extend the green from the stem up into the darker (shadow) areas of the flowers. Apply color with a toothpick wrapped tightly with cotton, following the shading in the flower. A very small amount of warm red (the same color as the bottom tulip) was used in the highlights of the top tulip, and yellow was used in the bottom tulip in the lighter areas. Using another color gives the flowers depth.

TIPS

○ Keep in mind that the same color oil paint can differ in appearance from manufacturer to manufacturer.

○ Layer colors for a more saturated look. Allow each layer to dry before adding another.

VARIATION

Build up colors for a textured look.

A heavier application of color was used for this variation. The color appears to sit on the surface, giving the image a bolder quality. The buildup of color also adds texture. The print surface was not prepared beforehand, so the colors stayed opaque.

1. Color the background using red oil applied with a cotton ball (use a cotton swab near the flower areas). Here, cadmium orange was used in the lighter areas of the background.
2. Using a cotton swab, apply dioxazine purple to the bottom tulip. Dab the color on without smoothing it in.
3. Apply cadmium orange to the top tulip with a cotton swab, and smooth it in a bit. Dab all over with a cotton ball, getting some of the color to go outside the lines of the flower. The feathering of orange in the background of this picture was created by the fibers from the cotton ball.
4. Use green to color in the stem, using the same technique as on the other stems.

△ Coloring the wispy clouds
adds mood and depth
to this photo.

◁ Oils work in expansive areas
(in this case, the sky and
sand dunes) as well as in
small areas (the kite and
its tail).

Hand Coloring Expansive Areas with Oils

GETTING STARTED

Prepare the print surface with either mineral spirits or the turpentine-and-oil solution, which is also used with colored pencils. (It's very important to use very small amounts of these solutions and to coat the print evenly.) Squirt a small amount of the oil colors that will be used to hand color the image onto a palette. You will be using the colors directly from the palette.

MATERIALS

- black-and-white print on matte-surface paper
- oils: sepia, ultramarine blue, cadmium orange, magenta, lemon yellow, crimson red, cadmium green, pink
- cotton balls
- toothpicks
- cotton swabs
- turpentine-and-oil solution
- blender pencil
- artist's palette
- transparent tape

SEPIA

LEMON YELLOW

ULTRAMARINE BLUE

CRIMSON RED

CADMIUM ORANGE

CADMIUM GREEN

MAGENTA

PINK

▷ **1**

Use a cotton swab to dab the sepia oil onto the dunes. With a fresh cotton swab, smooth the color in. Do not allow color to collect in areas. Keep using fresh cotton swabs until you have a smooth layer of color. If necessary, add more layers of color later for greater saturation.

◁ **2**

With a cotton swab, color the entire sky area and kite with ultramarine blue. Use circular motions to smooth it in. Don't worry about color bleeding into the clouds, fence, or kite.

TIP

○ Use the blender pencil to erase unwanted colors.

△ 3

Use a cotton swab to color the clouds in the upper-left portion of the photograph with cadmium orange, and smooth it in. For balance, use the same color for the clouds in the lower right. Use magenta for the cloud in the middle of the picture, applying the color with a cotton swab. For the wisps of clouds near the dunes, use lemon yellow applied with a toothpick wrapped in a small amount of cotton.

▷ **4**

After the paint has dried, go back into the clouds with the same colors and add another layer of color for a deeper, richer look. Gently run a toothpick dipped in water along the fencing to erase the blue color. Be careful not to scratch the print's surface. With a clean toothpick, do the same in the tail of the kite. Dip a clean toothpick wrapped in cotton in a small amount of water. With your fingers, squeeze out any excess water. Erase the blue in the kite. Notice that, without color, the kite and fencing stand out more.

VARIATION

Oil paints are ideal for textured detail work.

1. Prepare the print's surface by applying the turpentine-and-oil solution with a toothpick wrapped in a small amount of cotton. Use the solution very sparingly.
2. Prepare your palette.
3. Apply a small amount of lemon yellow to the kite with a toothpick wrapped in cotton. Apply crimson red with a fresh toothpick (not wrapped in cotton). Apply crimson red to one section of the kite's tail. Then, using the same procedure, add cadmium green and pink to the other sections of the tail.

CREATING SPECIAL EFFECTS

Now it's time to experiment and really play. You have a basic understanding of hand coloring and have learned with materials that are very forgiving, will erase easily, and are easy to apply to a print. This is your foundation. Now try mixing various mediums to create textures or even to totally obscure the image. Continue to avoid glossy paper. Remember that many mediums can be applied to a semimatte surface, but in order to use pencils, matte paper is still required. Most materials are either water-based (watercolor paints, retouching dyes, tempera, gouache, acrylics, pen and ink) or oil-based (oil paints, photo oils, oil sticks, oil pastels, oil-based markers). Other options include colored pencils, crayons, and markers. Some are transparent, and some are opaque. Different materials can be mixed, but be careful: The water-based materials can erase or dissolve pencils and oils, and the solvent used with pencils and oils can erase or dissolve watercolors. The gallery sections that follow offer many examples of different hand-coloring techniques—everything from using markers to making collages. No two look the same!

▽ Mix mediums to balance a textured background painted with acrylics and delicate subject matter colored with markers.

Markers

Markers are great fun to work with, and there are lots of varieties to choose from. There are water-based, solvent-based, or oil-based markers, and there are many colors and point ranges (from fine tip to broad tip). Markers are fairly permanent, so be sure that what you put down on paper is what you want. To thin the markers and make them easier to apply, try using a clear blender marker, which most art-supply stores carry. The blender also extends the ink's drying time, makes it somewhat transparent, and makes it possible to mix colors. Without the blender, the marker acts as an opaque medium and dries immediately. Rarely are markers used exclusively to hand color a photograph. Instead, they're usually used in just a section or two.

▽ *Bus Stop*
  by Amy Jean Rowan
  Rowan used oil pastels and a
  paint pen to color this image.

October 23 1997

Welcome to the World Paige Erin Gordon!

△ *October 23, 1997*
by Amy Jean Rowan
Rowan made a photocopy
of a Polaroid transfer and
colored it with markers.

△ *Ferris Wheel*
by Amy Jean Rowan
Rowan used a combination of
gesso, oil pastels, pastels, Conté
crayons, and a paint pen on this
color photograph.

From *Pastoral Interludes* series
by Kate and Geir Jordahl
The photographs in this series were hand
colored with colored pencils and acrylics.

Acrylics

Although acrylics come in a variety of
bold and vibrant colors, they can have a
flat appearance on a print. To avoid dull
color, thickly apply substantial amounts
of paint to create texture, or add another
medium on top of the acrylics. Before
they dry, acrylics are easy to remove with
water, but once dry (and they dry very
quickly), they're very durable. Normally,
acrylics are very opaque, but since they're
water-based, they can be combined with
water for a more transparent look.

◁ *Untitled*
by Laurie Klein
This cyanotype was made
from a glass positive found
at a flea market. A contact
print of it was made and
hand colored with water-
color pencil.

Watercolors

Watercolors are popular with hand colorists because they're translucent and can be used to create delicate washes of color. Tube watercolors produce deeper color than watercolor cakes, are easier to apply, and can be erased with small amounts of water. Liquid watercolors are very hard to remove and fade quickly, but they're incredibly vibrant in color. Watercolors in general work best on fiber-based paper. Apply watercolors with paintbrushes or cotton swabs, and prepare the colors on a palette. Also available are water-based crayons and pencils. These can be applied directly to a print and smoothed in with a cotton swab (or not smoothed in if texture is desired). Watercolors can often appear subtle, but layers can be added for greater intensity. Be sure to let each layer dry before adding another.

△ *Untitled*
by Jane Page-Conway
The artist first tones her photographs and
then hand colors them with watercolors.

△ *Untitled*
by Jane Page-Conway
The artist first tones her photographs and
then hand colors them with watercolors.

△ *Untitled*
  by Jane Page-Conway

Mixed Media

Many hand colorists use alternative film processes. Instead of making a silver photographic print, many make their own emulsions or buy premade emulsion and paint or coat a piece of paper with it. This process gives the print a handmade, tactile look, but the negative needs to be the size of the image you want to produce. Palladium and platinum printing are also quite popular. These prints have a silvery quality. Van Dyke prints are brownish in color, and cyanotypes are like blue prints. Very popular these days are Polaroid or image transfers that are transferred onto cold- or hot-pressed watercolor paper and then hand colored. Many artists create collages and integrate hand coloring into the piece. Collages can be created using a variety of materials, such as photocopies of old family snapshots, pictures cut out from magazines, old postcards, images that have been sewn together, or handmade paper or fabric.

△ *Untitled*
by Jane Page-Conway
This image was toned with a mix
of acrylics, oils, and pastels.

△ *Alyssa*
by Bobi Eldridge
Eldridge made a Polaroid transfer and then hand colored it with colored pencils and tempera.

△ *West Point Lighthouse*
by Bobi Eldridge
Eldridge made a Polaroid
transfer and then hand
colored it with colored
pencils and tempera.

Black and white photographs have been hand-tinted to add color since the beginning of photography. Create instant heirlooms by adding romantic colors to photos using SpotPen's Handcoloring Pens. These special pens are a convenient and neat way to make vintage tinted images and are specially formulated to penetrate the photo emulsion so that they can be used on matte or glossy finishes. Use a light application of colors for aged and subtle images, or intensify the coloration for modern, quirky looks.

hand-tinted
photographs

1 Tape the photograph to the work surface to prevent curling. In a disposable container, mix 2 cups water and 1/2 teaspoon Photo-Flo. Solution can be stored if covered.

2 Lightly moisten a sponge in the solution. Press the damp sponge two or three times against first area to be tinted until the photo-emulsion becomes tacky. Blot any excess solution with a paper towel or cotton ball.

3 With a light circular motion, rub presoftened pen over treated area to release color. Color intensity builds with application, but heavy pressure may scratch the emulsion. Colors may be layered; work with light tones first.

4 Repeat steps 2 and 3 to tint each area as desired. Even out excess dye by blotting with a moistened paper towel. The dye remover pen (which should also be presoftened) will correct minor mistakes, tone down colors, and soften or blend colors at the edges as long as the initial application of dye has not dried. Let dry 2 to 4 hours.

VARIATION
Color only one area of the photograph, such as a face, a flower, or an architectural detail, for a special effect.

MATERIALS
- black and white photographs
- SpotPen Handcoloring pens
- SpotPen Dye Remover pen
- Photo-Flo premoistening solution
- general craft supplies

Wire Photo Stand

This versatile photo stand can be created in minutes with wire and pliers. Refer to the diagram on page 293 for parts A–C.

MATERIALS
- 16 gauge black annealed wire
- needle-nose pliers
- diagram (page 293)
- 5/8" dowel or magic marker

Makes one photo stand

1 Wrap wire at one end two times around dowel or magic marker. With pliers, bend the long end of wire 90° from wire circles to create a stem. Wrap the short end of wire around the stem just below the coils and trim (A).

2 Shape the wire stem into a triangular shape similar to a coat hanger, wrapping end around stem where it re-joins at midpoint of stand (B). Extend the end to the back of the stand, creating an easel back. Coil the end with pliers and trim to finish (C).

TIPS
Presoften the pen tips following manufacturer's instructions before their first use or the pens may scratch the photo emulsion. If new images are printed specifically for tinting, ask for them to be developed 10 percent lighter than normal for a background more receptive to the addition of color. Prints made on resin-coated paper will retain their form better. Fiber-based paper may curl when colored, requiring dry-mount pressing after completion. Read the manufacturer's inserts for more information on choosing a developing paper.

Journal Techniques

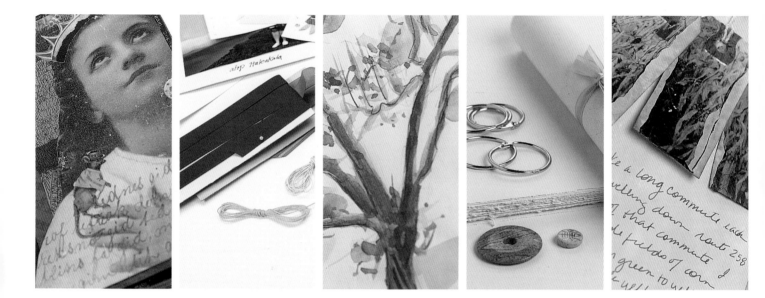

Advanced journal techniques such as those found in the following chapters can help make your journal something special. Projects such as image transfers and photo-emulsion lifts will help you design visually stunning pages.

The books you create should reflect your personal vision and esthetic sense, whether that be funky or arty, crafty or flowery. Like different painters using the same paints, these techniques can be utilized to create many different looks and designs, and they can be used by those of us just learning to be artistic and seasoned journalers alike. And if something doesn't work out right the first time, you can always turn the page and start again.

transferring photocopies to cloth

emulsion

Tea was poured onto the front and back of this completed photo emulsion to enhance the color of the pears and create a patina.

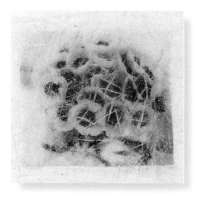

transfer

An acrylic transfer of anemones takes on a rugged, earthy feel when placed on a nubbly cotton gauze. The image was then sliced with a razor blade and stretched to further fracture its lines.

Photos to Fabric

- Select a picture to be transferred to fabric and make a color photocopy of it. Keep in mind that the finished image will be a mirrored version of the original. Carefully cut out the portion of the photocopy to be transferred.

- Place the photocopy face up on a sheet of wax paper and brush a generous coat of the fabric transfer medium over it. Carefully lift the image off the wax paper and place it face down on the white fabric. Press down firmly.

- Allow the medium to dry thoroughly. Soak the fabric in water and gently rub off the paper. Cut out the portions of the image to be used and adhere them to the green fabric using the fabric transfer medium as glue.

crafter's tips

- An easy way to remove a photo emulsion from a cold water bath is to slip a piece of wax paper beneath it. Hold two corners of the emulsion in place and use the motion of the water to adjust the image as you want it to appear on the finished piece.

- Wet the fabric before you place an emulsion on it. This will make it easier to adjust the image after it has been transferred.

- To quickly transfer a photograph to fabric, take your image to a photocopy shop that can put the picture onto heat transfer paper. When you get home, all you have to do is iron the photo into place.

- fabric transfer medium
- color photocopy of a photograph
- paintbrush
- wax paper
- water
- white fabric
- green fabric
- scissors
- tray

Treasured fine art photos take on new life when displayed on an unexpected medium. Try overlapping or mirroring images, or cut a photograph into pieces before arranging it on the material.

The type of fabric used will affect a piece's finished look. Keep in mind the feel you are trying to convey as you choose your materials.

Photo transfers offer varied means of expression. Choose the technique that suits you and your project best. Photo emulsions produce a more subdued color palette than photo transfers do.

attaching emulsions to fabric

Photo Emulsions

- Take a slide of your chosen image to a photographer or photo printing store and have them make a print of it using Polaroid film type 669, 59, 559, or 809. This is different from the standard Polaroid instant camera film you may have at home.

- Set up your equipment near the stove, using items that you will never eat from. Prepare a pan of cold water and bring a pot of water to a boil. You should be wearing gloves to protect your hands during this process.

- Submerge the photo in the pot and simmer it for three or four minutes. Use a pair of tongs to remove the photograph and immediately place it in the pan of cold water.

- While the photograph is in the water, use your gloved finger-tips to gently push the image from the edges of the print to remove it from the backing of the photograph.

- Once the backing has been removed, only the emulsion should be floating in the water. Carefully remove it and place it on your fabric. Be sure to smooth out air bubbles and excess water. The emulsion can be manipulated to fold over itself, stretch, tear, etc., to suit your design needs.

- Hang the fabric up to dry, weighting down the bottom with clothespins to ensure that the fabric dries straight.

- color print
- tight-fitting rubber gloves
- shallow pan
- cooking pot
- water
- metal tongs
- fabric
- stove
- clothespins

Image Transfers

MATERIALS

xylene solvent

bone folder

can with a lid

rags

respirator, face mask, or fan

binder clips

Note: The chemicals used in these steps can be toxic. Read all manufacturer's safety precautions before attempting these techniques.

Though the process is essentially the same as using a blender pen, using solvents to transfer images from photocopies is more involved, allows better control over the transfer, and results in a more distinct image that is less wispy. Artist Lori Kay Ludwig uses solvents to render photographs more intimate. This technique allows the repeated use of images without the need for a darkroom and permits her to be more involved with the image than a traditional photograph might.

I CREATED THIS BOOK TO RECORD MY TRANSITION TO MOTHERHOOD. IT CONTAINS IMPORTANT VISUAL RECORDS OF MY PERSONAL AND EMOTIONAL DEVELOPMENT.

Artist: Lori Kay Ludwig

6 MONTHS

Changing faster now...
skin is becoming ironi
even my FACE has gained
weight...
seems as though puberty
is bigger every morning
wonder what after will be?

baby do to my life?
...disappear...
...about...

SEVEN MONTHS

Step by Step:

ONE

TWO

THREE

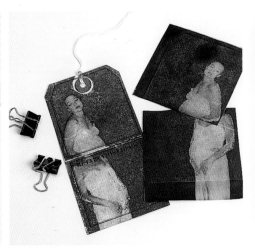

STEP ONE **PREPARE YOUR SUPPLIES** Pour about two inches of xylene into a can with a lid. Make sure your rags and burnishing tool are handy. Wear rubber gloves and a respirator, and use a fan in a well-ventilated area, or work outside. Place your photo-copied image face-down onto the page and clip into place with binder clips.

STEP ONE **APPLY THE SOLVENT** Dip the rag into the can. The rag should be thoroughly wet but not dripping. Rub the solvent onto the backside of your photo-copy, covering a small section of the image at a time. Burnish each section as you go with your burnishing tool. Take a peek every so often to see which areas need to be burnished again. Don't be surprised if you need to apply solvent to or burnish an area a few times before you achieve the desired effect.

STEP THREE **REMOVE THE PHOTO-COPY** Remove the binder clips and peel away the photocopy. In some places, the toner may have adhered the paper, leaving tiny, thin, threadlike bits on the image when the pho-tocopy is peeled back. This is considered an advantage, as it lends a hand-drawn appear-ance to your final image. You can now enhance the image with colored pencils, charcoal, pastel, watercolor—whatever works best with your own journal.

Some journals are kept in chronological order, starting on the first page and ending on the last page, while some have entries arbitrarily entered throughout the book. If you're intimidated by the first blank page in a book, try creating your first entry somewhere in the middle of the book, or start your journal the same way every time. For example, you might always begin your journal with a page describing who you are, where you are, and how you obtained or made the book: what fabric you used, how long it took to bind, where you made it. You might also write about the last journal you kept, how much time it spanned, and what you liked about it. After you've made the first entry, you'll feel less apprehensive about the prospect of all those blank pages.

The images in this book were found vacation photos discovered in antique shops. All the images show cobblestones in them. Artist: Roberta Lavadour

notes:

Always use solvents such as xylene in a well-ventilated area, either inside with a fan on and the windows open, or outdoors.

Other solvents besides xylene will work to transfer images, and can also produce results of a different opacity and hue. Try this technique using acetone, lighter fluid, hairspray, peppermint oil, or denatured alcohol.

Try adding transfer images from a special trip into a travel journal, baby pictures into a new baby journal, or pictures of friends and family into a daily journal to document the people in your life.

Emulsion Lifts

MATERIALS

camera that uses
pack film

pack film

candy thermometer

tea kettle

glass or Pyrex trays
to hold water

contact or shelf paper

scissors

wax paper

clear-coat spray enamel

brayer or bone folder

An exciting and advanced technique for adding photographic imagery to your journals is a process called an emulsion lift. This involved process requires lifting or removing the very delicate emulsion from photograph paper and then adhering it to your journal pages. One of the nice results of this technique is that the transferred emulsion is so thin that you can barely feel that it's there, but the image remains vivid and crisp. Lori Kay Ludwig uses emulsion lifts extensively in her journals. In the example here, she has utilized an altered book to create a journal documenting the changing of the seasons which contains emulsion lifts almost exclusively, even on the cover.

I CREATED THIS ONE-OF-A-KIND ARTISTS' BOOK TO RECORD THE MONTH OF OCTOBER 1999.

Artist: Lori Kay Ludwig

BELOW: This is a solvent transfer. BOTTOM: This emulsion-lift monthly journal is a hand-bound, recycled arithmetic book from 1852.

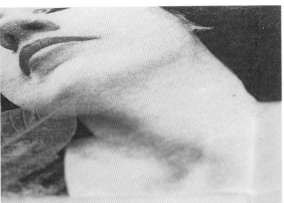

Step by Step:

EMULSION LIFTS

ONE

TWO

STEP ONE **HEAT THE WATER** Note that this process only works with cameras that use pack film, a special film by Polaroid that is the only type of film that works with this technique. Ask your local camera shop for more information regarding cameras that use this type of film. Pour a tea kettle's worth of water that is exactly 160 degrees Fahrenheit (71 degrees Celsius) into the tray. Carefully monitor the water's temperature with the thermometer. Adhere contact or shelf paper to the back of the photograph to prevent the backing of the print from dissolving in the water.

STEP TWO **IMMERSE THE PHOTO-GRAPH IN WATER** Submerge your photograph in the water for approximately four minutes. During this time, you should start to see bubbles form underneath the image, and the edges will start to loosen. Gently rock the tray if necessary to hasten the process.

THREE

FOUR

STEP THREE **REMOVE THE EMULSION**
When the emulsion starts to peel away from the photograph, carefully float the emulsion on top of a clean sheet of wax paper and flatten any wrinkles or creases. Next, carefully remove the wax paper and the emulsion from the water.

STEP FOUR **PLACE THE EMULSION INTO YOUR JOURNAL** Carefully lift the thin layer of emulsion off the wax paper and place it onto your journal page. It may crease, crinkle, or even tear. Be prepared to accept these effects as part of your composition. Press the image lightly with a brayer to remove any water or air bubbles from beneath its surface and seal with a spray enamel.

notes:

This process creates very vivid and clear images in such an unusual way that you should consider using the images for special pages or even the cover of your journal.

Try playing around with the way the emulsion crinkles and folds as it is transferred.

The ethereal effect of emulsion-lift transfers looks great in dream journals!

P·h·o·t·o M·a·i·l·e·r·s

*A*lthough photo mailers appear complicated, they are easy to make; think of them as paper packages holding wonderful images inside. This unique style of card works as both a card and a photograph frame. Small photo mailers are perfect as baby announcements and can be made to the size of any picture. Tailor this card to many different occasions by choosing various papers. Do not limit yourself to photographs when designing a photo mailer. Window photo mailers take a little more work to construct, but can be used to frame small three-dimensional items, such as seashells, keys, or dried flowers, depending on the occasion.

P·h·o·t·o M·a·i·l·e·r I·n·s·p·i·r·a·t·i·o·n·s

☺ You will have gold pieces by the bushel. ☺

Chinatown

NOB HILL

Union Square

POWELL ST. STATION

Old U.S. Mint

LA MANO

Use festive paper to create a birthday theme, or white and gold papers for an elegant wedding invitation. Decorate the cover of the photo mailer with a collage, special mementos, or images cut from books and magazines. You can build a paper "inspirations" file by collecting everyday items such as stamps, photographs, ticket stubs, playbills, subway maps, wine labels (especially exotic ones), cookie fortunes, travel brochures, road maps, shopping bags, and calendars.

Other finds — buttons, flat beads, coins, dried flowers — are treasures that can double as decorations.

Paper selection is important, especially if you are working with glue for the first time. Thin paper, such as pages from a magazine or wrapping paper, may curl or wrinkle; thick handmade papers will be difficult to work with at the corners. Choose medium-weight papers, such as marbled, Japanese, paste paper, or printed paper.

Mourvèdre

Basic Photo Mailer

T his special card combines many of the techniques already presented in the previous chapters. Prepare all the materials before you start to glue. Choose papers for the outside of the cover, the interior, and the binding strip. Measure the papers and then cut out each piece. Once the first few steps have been completed, the corners require special attention. You may want to practice making them a few times before attempting the final project.

Materials

- Two pieces of illustration board, 4" x 6" (10 cm x 15 cm)
- Two pieces of decorative paper for the outside, 5" x 7" (13 cm x 18 cm)
- Two pieces of decorative paper for the inside, 3 ¾" x 5 ¾" (9.5 cm x 14.5 cm)
- Piece of paper for the binding strip (use the same paper as on the inside),
      1 ¼" x 6" (3 cm x 15 cm)
- Piece of writing paper or a photograph, 3 ½" x 5 ½" (9 cm x 14 cm)
- Black photo corners
- Craft knife
- Metal ruler
- Pencil
- PVA glue
- Glue brush
- Bone folder
- Cutting mat

❖**1** Lay the paper for the outside cover pattern-side down. Measure ½" (1 cm) from all edges and mark this border with the pencil. Apply glue to cover the square area inside the pencil lines, then center the illustration board and gently adhere it to the glued surface, using the pencil marks as a guide.

❖**2** Turn the glued piece over. With the side of your thumb or the bone folder, press firmly from the center out to the edges to create a smooth surface. Rub the entire surface with your fingers until the paper is flat and wrinkle-free.

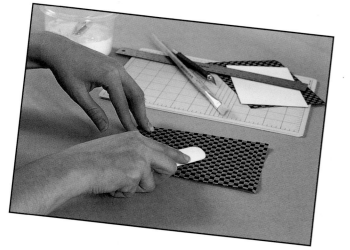

❖**3** Turn the card back over. Apply glue to the long flaps of paper on the right and left edges. Fold the flaps firmly over the illustration board and smooth them with your thumb or the bone folder. Press the paper flat only to the top and bottom edges of the illustration board. Be careful not to press the paper together at the corners where it extends beyond the board.

❖**4** Apply glue to the top corners of the paper. Fold the corner paper at a 45-degree angle toward the center of the board. Crease the paper and press down. Press in the excess paper created by the angle fold along the top edge of the illustration board. Repeat with the bottom corners.

❖**5** Apply glue to the remaining short strips of paper at the top and bottom edges of the boards. Fold them over the illustration board and smooth them with a bone folder or your fingers. Make sure that the paper does not hang over the edge of the board.

❖**6** Apply glue to the back of the contrasting paper. Work from the center out, covering the entire surface and all edges. Center the paper on the illustration board and press to adhere. One half of the card is now complete. Repeat steps 1 through 6 to make the other side of the card.

To prevent the illustration board from warping as the glue dries, put a sheet of paper between the sides of the finished card so they will not stick to each other, and press the card under a pile of heavy books.

❖**7** Place one card on top of the other, with the contrasting papers facing each other. Apply glue to the back of the binding strip, covering the entire surface. Place one half of the glued strip on the left side of the top card.

❖**8** Stand the card upright on its right edge. Square the covers, matching the edges evenly all the way around. Use your thumb and forefinger to roll the binding strip firmly around the two boards to the back card.

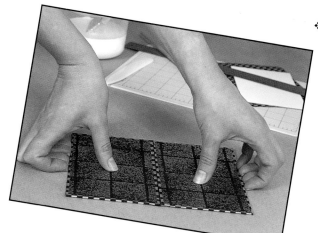

❖*9* Open the card and lay it flat, with the outside covers facing down. Press the right and left edges of the card toward the center to catch the glued strip between the two boards. Hold the cards for about a minute until the glue sets. The card should open and close easily as if on a hinge.

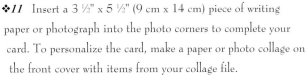

❖*10* Position two photo corners on the left and right top corners of the 3 ½" x 5 ½" (9 cm x 14 cm) paper. Apply glue to the back of the corners. Press the corners onto the inside of the card at an equal distance from the top edges. Slide the paper out and repeat this procedure with the bottom corners. If you want a double frame, apply corners to the other side of the card as well.

❖*11* Insert a 3 ½" x 5 ½" (9 cm x 14 cm) piece of writing paper or photograph into the photo corners to complete your card. To personalize the card, make a paper or photo collage on the front cover with items from your collage file.

Variation

Choose paper to complement the photograph you want to send. Dress up a child's photo with playful, colorful papers from different countries and glue tiny toys or objects to the front of the card.

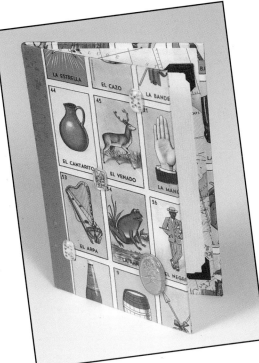

Baby Photo Mailer

The baby photo mailer is a perfect card to welcome a little one into the world, but this type of card can be used for any occasion. Select papers and ribbon appropriate for your design, and cut them to the required sizes. Glue the paper to the boards, add the ribbon, and bind the boards together. For a double frame, you can apply picture corners on both sides of the card.

Materials

- Two pieces of illustration board or cardboard, 3" x 3" (7.5 cm x 7.5 cm)
- Two pieces of decorative paper for the outside, 4" x 4" (10 cm x 10 cm)
- Two pieces of contrasting decorative paper for the inside, 2 ¾" x 2 ¾" (7 cm x 7 cm)
- Piece of paper for the binding strip (use the same paper as on the inside), 1" x 3" (2.5 cm x 7.5 cm)
- Piece of writing paper, 2 ½" x 2 ½" (6.5 cm x 6.5 cm)
- Length of ribbon, 8 ½" (21 cm)
- Picture corners
- Craft knife
- Metal ruler
- Pencil
- PVA glue
- Glue brush
- Bone folder
- Cutting mat

❖*1* Apply glue to the back of the paper for the outside cover. Center the illustration board on the paper, leaving approximately ½" (1 cm) on all sides. Turn the card over. Use your fingers to smooth the paper over the board. Start at the center and work out to the edges.

Brush the glue evenly, taking care not to use too much because it will cause the paper to tear, especially in the corners. Also, if the glue leaks out, it will stain the ribbon and paper.

❖*2* Turn the card over again. Apply glue to the right and left flaps. Fold the flaps over the illustration board and smooth the paper with your fingers. Do not press the paper at the top and bottom edges together; they will be folded at an angle for the corners in the next step.

❖*3* Apply glue to the top corner flaps. For each corner, pull the top piece of folded paper to a 45-degree angle. It is important to angle the fold so that the paper will not hang over the edge. Tuck any excess paper toward the board edge. Repeat on the bottom corners.

❖*4* Apply glue to the top and bottom flaps and adhere them to the board. Make sure that the folded corner is glued on the inside of the board edge. Now repeat steps 1 through 4 for the other side of the card.

❖5 Lay the card pieces side by side with the outside covers facing down. Cut the ribbon in half, and add glue to one of the pieces of ribbon, ¼" (.5 cm) away from its end. Glue the ribbon to the middle of the outside edge of one card. To position the ribbon in the same place on the other card, close the card, lay the second piece on top of the first, and make a mark. Glue the second length of ribbon to the other card.

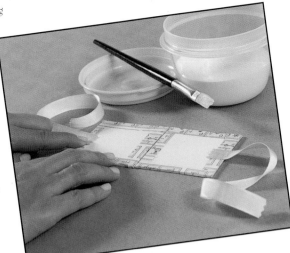

❖6 Lay the contrasting papers right side down. Brush glue from the center out to the edges. Center and adhere the papers to the inside of the cards. Use your thumb or a bone folder to smooth the paper flat.

Match the placement of the ribbons, one on top of the other, so the card will tie properly.

❖7 Place one card on top of the other, with the outside covers facing out and all the edges meeting. Apply glue to the back of the binding strip. Place half of the glued strip evenly on the front left side of the top card. Roll the paper over the edges and adhere it to the back of the card.

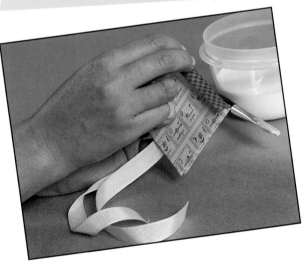

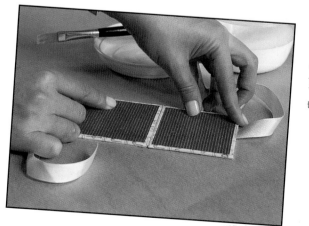

❖8 Open the card flat. Press the left and right edges of the card toward the center to catch the binding strip between the boards. Hold the cards about a minute until the glue sets.

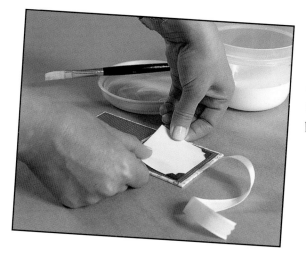

❖9 Place the photo corners on the left and right top corners of the 2 ½" x 2 ½" (6.5 cm x 6.5 cm) writing paper. Apply glue to the back of the corners, center them, and press them onto the inside of the card.
Slide the paper out and repeat the procedure with the bottom corners.

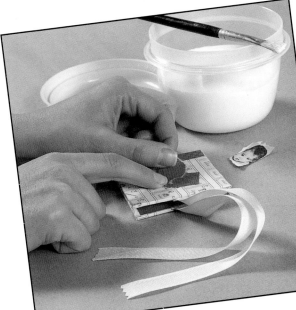

❖10 Make a collage on the front cover with complementary papers. Glue a baby photo for a final layer over the collage.

Variations

For more sophisticated photo mailers, make the paper and the binding all the same color. Add a button that closes the photo mailer with string. Simply glue the button to the top of a glass bead that is then glued to the card. The bead gives the button height to wrap the string around the base.

Keepsake Photo Mailer

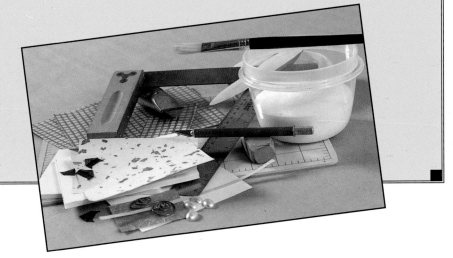

T ailor this versatile card to suit almost any occasion. Measure the foam core and outside paper to make the window, then remove the window. Cover the foam core and line the window frame with paper. Glue a piece of paper or a photograph behind the window to serve as a backdrop for your object. Cover the other piece of foam core, then bind the two pieces together. Add picture corners and decorate the window.

Materials

- Two pieces of ¼" (.5 cm) foam core, 4" x 5" (10 cm x 13 cm)
- Two pieces of decorative paper for the outside, 5 ½" x 6 ½" (14 cm x 16 cm)
- Two pieces of decorative paper for the inside, 3 ¾" x 4 ¾" (9.5 cm x 11.5 cm)
- Strip of paper for window lining, ¼" x 7" (.5 cm x 18 cm)
- Piece of card stock or firm paper for behind the window, 3 ½" x 4 ½" (8.5 cm x 12 cm)
- Piece of decorative paper, photograph, or image for the window, 2" x 2 ½" (5 cm x 6.5 cm)
- Piece of paper for the binding strip (use the same paper as on the outside), 4" x 2" (10 cm x 5 cm)
- Object for the window and four picture corners
- T-square
- Eraser
- Craft knife
- Metal ruler
- Pencil
- PVA glue
- Glue brush
- Bone folder
- Cutting mat

❖**1**   Lay one piece of the foam core on your work surface. Measure and mark with the pencil 1 ¼" (3 cm) from the left and right edges, then measure and mark 1 ½" (4 cm) from the top and bottom edges. Make straight lines with the T-square at the marks to form the shape of the window. Use the T-square as a guide as you cut out the window with the craft knife.

Cut the foam core several times before moving the ruler to ensure that the blade is all the way through.

Draw arrows on the paper and the foam core to use as placement guides.

❖**2**   Make a line ¾" (2 cm) from all edges on the back of the outside paper. Position the foam core within the lines. Hold the foam core in place and use the pencil to trace around the inner edges of the window. Center the piece of card stock under the window and trace around the inner edges of the window again.

Cut from corner to corner for clean edges.

❖**3**   Remove the foam core and the card stock. On the outside paper, measure ½" (1 cm) from each side of the window outline to form a smaller square. Use the metal ruler and craft knife to cut out the inner square. Then cut a diagonal from each window corner to the corner of the inner square to create flaps.

❖4 Apply glue to the back of the outside paper. Center the foam core on the paper within the marked lines and adhere it. Turn the foam core over and smooth the paper with your hand. Pull the flaps gently through the window in the foam core toward the back of the card.

❖5 Apply glue to the left and right flaps along the length of the card. Fold the flaps over the edges and adhere them to the foam core. Glue only as far as the top and bottom edges of the foam core. Glue the paper between the folded flaps at the corners onto the top edge of the foam core.

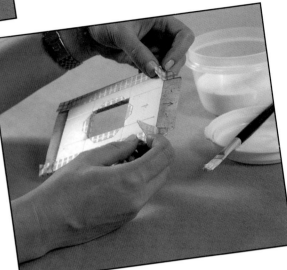

❖6 Glue the back flap over the top edge toward the front flap. Apply glue and fold both flaps over the top edge toward the back of the foam core. Repeat these steps at the bottom edge of the card.

❖7 Apply glue to the back of the ¼" (.5 cm) paper strip. Insert the paper strip at the lower left corner and along the edges of the window. Push it into the corners tightly for an accurate fit. Trim any excess. Use the bone folder to work the paper into the corners and smooth the edges.

Check the length of the paper strip to make sure it fits before applying the glue.

❖*8*   Center and glue the 2" x 2 ½" (5 cm x 6.5 cm) window paper onto the card stock over the pre-traced square. Apply glue to the front of the card stock around the window paper. Adhere the front of the card stock to the back of the foam core, so that the window paper appears in the window.

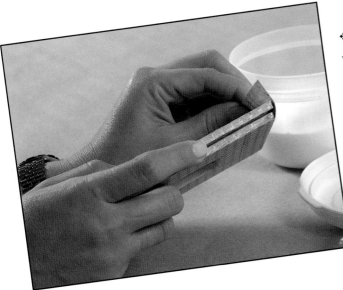

❖*9*   Apply glue to the back of the inside paper. Center the paper over the card stock on the foam core and adhere it. Smooth the paper flat with your hands. Create the other side of the card following the previous steps, eliminating the construction of the window.

❖*10*   Place one side of the card on top of the other, with the inside papers facing each other. Apply glue to the back of the binding strip. Put half of the glued strip on the front left side of the top card. Pull the other half of the binding strip around the foam core edges to the outside edge of the bottom card.

❖*11*   Open the card and lay it flat with the outside covers facing down. Press the right and left edges of the card toward the center to catch the glued strip between the two pieces of foam core. Let the glue set for about a minute. To finish the card, add the picture corners (see the instructions given for the Basic Photo Mailer on page 234) and your window object.

Making Frames
& Photos Albums

Forever Friends Photo Box

A golden moment captured on film is what this photo box is all about. Following childhood and preceding adulthood, we develop some of our most cherished relationships that will endure throughout our lives. If we do happen to lose touch with them, this project will preserve the memory just as you left it. Choose one classic image that relays the extraordinary feeling of serendipitously showing off youthful grins, gorgeous figures, and spiffy clothes. Splurge on a fancy frame, glass beads, and floral roses to enhance the beauty of your visual time capsule.

Materials

Old photo of a gathering of friends

6" × 8" × 1½" (15 cm × 20 cm × 4 cm) wood box

10" × 8½" (25 cm × 22 cm) wood frame

3" × 5" (8 cm × 13 cm) wood block with scalloped edge

Bag of glass seed beads

4 medium-sized fabric or dried roses

Bottle of translucent squeeze glitter

Acrylic paints in black, white, and gold

Stencil brush

Picture-hanging attachment

Basic craft supplies

1) Paint the box white and the frame black. When dry, stencil gold on top of both and let dry. Squeeze the translucent glitter on both surfaces and gently sweep it across with the brush to create a shimmery effect.

2) Copy an old photo in color and use a glue stick to adhere it to the wood block. Paint the ridges black and stencil with gold. Working on top of newspaper, line the top edge of the block with industrial-strength craft glue. Sprinkle the seed beads and then pat them with your finger to create an even layer. This will reduce the number of beads that will fall off. Tap the block on the paper to catch loose beads. Let it dry and then attach the block to the center of the wood box.

3) Rest the picture frame over the front of the box and line it up evenly. Hold it firmly and turn it upside down. Run a bead of hot glue along the seams where the frame and box meat to secure it and let dry.

4) Adhere a layer of seed beads around the outer edge of the frame. Glue one rose to each corner of the frame. Add a hanging attachment to the back.

TIP

Take extra care when lining up the frame with the box to ensure the two are sealed in a straight and even manner. Lightly tap box to remove loose seed beads. Gently remove any stragglers by hand or with tweezers.

VARIATION

The color scheme of this box was created for an old black-and-white photo. If using a color photo, change colors to match. Add small keepsakes around the border that are associated with the picture.

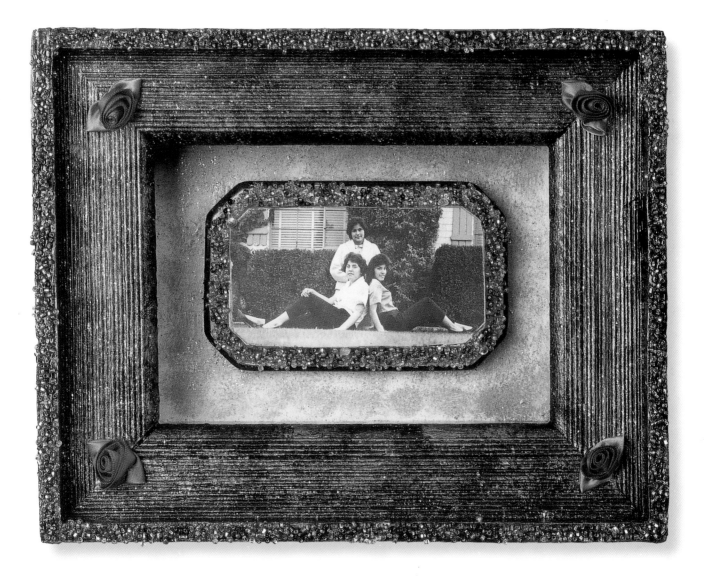

Dimensions 6" X 8" (15 cm X 20 cm)

Artist Kathy Cano-Murillo

These custom-sized frames are perfect for a series of related photos or small items

such as pressed flowers, stamps, or drawings. Intricate cut patterns, like the corners

on these frames, can be produced effortlessly using paper-edging scissors, which cut

through veneer easily. Many effects are possible with the wide variety of decorative

edging scissors available.

suspended
veneer frames

starting out:

Determine the size of the frame based on the size of the image to be used. The frames seen here are 4" (10 cm) square, with a 1" (3 cm) border around the 2" (5 cm) square picture opening. Wood veneer can be found at craft supply and woodworking stores, often in assorted packs of 8 1/2" x 11" (22 cm x 28 cm) sheets. Avoid using oak veneer, which is very hard and can splinter when cut with paper edgers.

MATERIALS

- wood veneer in
  contrasting colors
- acetate (optional)
- pictures of choice
- embroidery floss or string
- wooden beads
- quick-grab adhesive
- glue stick
- spray acrylic sealer or
  varnish
- masking tape
- decorative corner edging
  scissors
- 1/8" (3 mm) hole punch
- craft knife

1 **Cut and punch the veneer.** Measure, mark, and use a craft knife to cut out two pieces of veneer in contrasting colors. Cut out the center opening as well. Next, use corner-edging scissors on one of the pieces of veneer to cut all four corners. Lay this trimmed piece on top of the second piece of veneer, and tape the two together. Punch holes in the top and bottom center of the frame. Repeat this procedure to make as many frames as desired. Then, remove the tape and lay all the veneer frames on a piece of newspaper and finish with a few quick, short bursts of spray sealer or varnish, if desired. Use the spray in a well-ventilated area or outdoors.

2 **Place the pictures in the frames.** If a protective cover is desired, cut out pieces of acetate 1/4" (6 mm) larger than the opening of the frames. Use a glue stick to adhere the acetate to the decorative-edged veneer. Position the image as desired, and secure with tape or other adhesive. Next, use quick-grab adhesive to glue the top and back frame pieces together.

QUICK TIPS

For added detail, position the grain of the wood intentionally when assembling the frames. In all the tops of the frames seen here, the grain is vertical, and in all the back pieces the grain is horizontal.

When selecting the beads, make sure a single knot is enough to prevent the beads from slipping. If not, try a thicker string or beads with smaller holes.

3 **String the frames together.** Arrange the frames on a table spacing them out as desired for the finished project. Use this layout to roughly measure and cut a length of embroidery floss, string, or cord twice as long as the layout, plus 12" (30 cm) extra. Next, bring both ends of the string together, and then make a knot in the opposite end leaving a small loop for hanging. Slip a wooden bead up to the knot, then make another knot under it to keep in place. Be sure to use beads larger than the holes punched in the veneer. Thread another bead on the string. Then, bring the string through the front of the top hole in the first frame, down the back of the frame, and out through the bottom hole; add another bead. Make knots in the string around each bead to keep them from slipping, making sure the string is taut against the back of the frame. Continue until each frame is attached.

SHORTCUT/VARIATION:
Make the frames double sided to create a photo mobile. Use two pieces of veneer for each frame, but adhere them back to back. Slip in images back to back as well. Instead of trimming the frame corners with corner edgers, trim each side of the frame with edging scissors for a decorative finish.

Baby's First Year
Photo Memory Album

THE WHIMSICAL WRAPAROUND DESIGN *on our album cover started out as a wallpaper border. Make a quick trip to any major home improvement outlet and you'll find a number of nursery wall borders that are the perfect size for embellishing an album. Our sample piece is a die-cut design; for a coordinated look, try a piece left over from decorating baby's room. The other specialty item you'll need is handmade paper. It comes in a wide variety of colors, textures, and styles and is available at most art supply stores. Or you might try creating your own decorative papers. This is such an easy cut-and-glue project, you'll want to make several. For a different effect, try the project variation. Most proud parents need more than one volume to do justice to the most beautiful baby in the world.*

Materials:

8" x 8½" (20 cm x 27 cm) photo album

22" x 30" (56 cm x 76 cm) textured paper

24" (61 cm) length of wall border

Extra-thick white craft glue

1" (3 cm) foam brush

Scissors

Ruler

Instructions

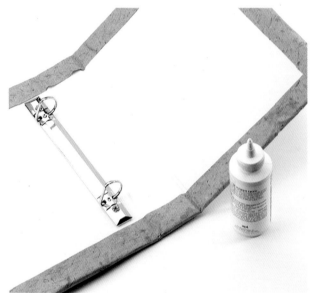

1. Open the album and lay it flat on the textured paper. Cut 1½" (4 cm) beyond the edge of the album all around. Fold the paper margins to the inside of the album, creasing the edges to measure for a snug fit. Remove the album from the paper. Apply a bead of glue around the edges of the album's spine and smooth the textured paper into position. In the same way, glue the paper to the album front cover and back cover. Work with the album in the closed position to ensure that the textured paper doesn't bind or restrict the album's opening and closing.

2. Apply a bead of glue on one inside edge of the album. Spread the glue evenly with a 1" (3 cm) foam brush. Gently fold the paper over, pressing it into place. Fold and glue the opposite edge in the same way. Trim diagonally at the corners and cut away the excess paper to reduce bulk. Glue down the remaining two sides. Let dry for at least one hour.

A Word About
A Sticky Situation

Choose a glue that is capable of adhering diverse surfaces such as plastic to paper, metal to fabric, and the like. A good thick white glue that becomes tacky immediately and dries clear will make your projects go smoothly and will ensure the professional results you desire.

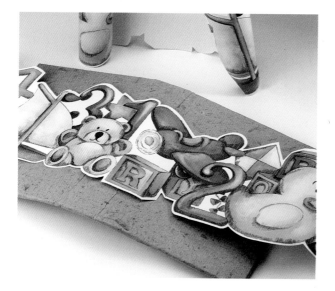

3. Open the album and lay it cover side up. Lay the wall border across it, adjusting its position so that an appropriate design falls on the front cover. Cut the wall border 1½" (4 cm) beyond the album edges at each end. Brush glue evenly on the wrong side of the wall border. Smooth the border into place around the album cover and onto the inside edges. As in step 1, work with the album in a closed position.

4. Measure the inside front and back covers. Cut a piece of textured paper for each. Trim the three outside edges by about ¼" (.5 cm). Test-fit each piece, and retrim if necessary. Using a foam brush, apply glue to the underside of the paper and spread it evenly. Press the papers into position. Let dry.

Variation

For a fabric-covered album, pad the cover first by gluing on several layers of plump quilt batting. The overall procedure is the same as for a paper cover. The key is to plan where the printed design will fall and to cut the fabric on-grain. If a fabric is loosely woven or tends to fray, a fusible tricot backing will stabilize it while maintaining flexibility. The ribbon ties are glued to the inside covers before the protective paper covering is added.

Wedding Photo Album

BASED ON A PROJECT BY RAVEN REGAN

R aven Regan enjoys making this style of book because it can be customized for any purpose. It measures 9" x 11 $^1/_4$" (23 cm x 28.5 cm), so standard 8 $^1/_2$" x 11" (22 cm x 28 cm) paper fits perfectly inside. The weight of the pages can vary from a quality bond for a guest book, to a card stock for a photo album, to handmade paper for a gardener's journal. The covers are equally versatile, with papers, ribbons, or patterns used as decoration. Regan personalizes her wedding books by using colors and ribbons she knows the bride likes and by including an invitation to the wedding on the cover—and perhaps even using a quotation of significance to the couple.

What You Need

Two pieces decorative cover paper measuring 10 $^1/_2$" x 11" (27 cm x 28 cm) each

Two pieces binding cloth measuring 11" x 5" (28 cm x 13 cm) each

Two pieces endpaper measuring 9 $^1/_8$" x 8 $^1/_2$" (23 cm x 22 cm) each

Two pieces Mill board measuring 9" x 11" (23 cm x 28 cm)

29 pages measuring 8 $^1/_2$" x 11" (22 cm x 28 cm)

Ribbon

PVA glue

29 pages gold-stamped vellum paper

Scissors

Utility knife

Clamps

1" (3 cm) foam glue brush

Drill

Bone folder

Large-eye needle

Glue stick

Metal ruler

Pencil

Decorations for cover: gold no-hole beads, glitter, and charms

Gold photo corners

Gold marker

step-by-step

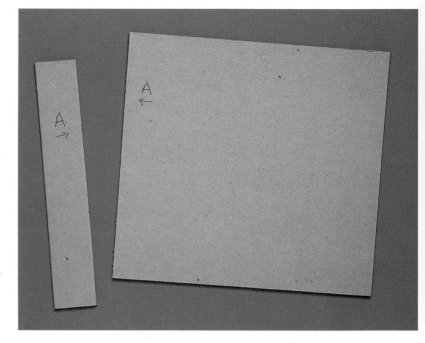

1. Cutting the covers

Cut two pieces of Mill board to 9" x 11" (23 cm, x 28 cm), and then cut a 9" x 1 ¹/₂" (23 cm x 4 cm) strip from each of these cover boards. Use the smaller strips for the spine.

2. Covering the boards

Thin some PVA glue with water, making it the consistency of coffee cream. Then use a 1" (3 cm) sponge brush to apply the glue to the back of each cover board and adhere them to the inside of the decorative paper. Make the boards flush on the binding side (the left side) and centered, with equal margins of paper on the other three sides. Then fold the cloth over and turn the two corners in at a 45-degree angle; glue the paper to the board. Finally, glue the endpapers to each board.

3. Adding binding cloth to covers

To create the hinge of the book, lay out an 11" x 5" (28 cm x 13 cm) piece of book-binding cloth and position the cover and spine on it about $^1/_4$" (.5 cm) apart. Glue the boards to the cloth, and fold the cloth over to completely encase the spine and the edge of the cover. Repeat this process for the back cover.

4. Making the pages

To make the pages fold back easily, score each one 1 $^3/_4$" (4.5 cm) in from the left at the spine with a bone folder. If necessary, add spacers at the spine measuring 8 $^1/_2$" x 1 $^1/_2$" (22 cm x 4 cm) cut from the same paper as the pages.

5. Binding the book

To use a Japanese side-sewn binding, as Regan did here, mark and drill five holes along the spine (through the cover boards, pages, and spacers, which you should clamp together to keep them from moving). Make the end holes 1" (3 cm) in from the top and bottom (or head and tail) of the book. The other holes should be 1 ³/₄" (4.5 cm) apart. Indent all the holes ³/₄" (2 cm) from the binding edge, then sew the book together with ribbon.

6. Decorating the cover and pages

Embellish the decorative-paper cover with cut-out hearts, ribbon, gold photo corners, and charms. For the inside, add photos with gold photo corners and text written in gold marker.

Variation

9" x 11 ¼" (23 cm x 28.5 cm)

To make a different book using the same
structure and binding, add a framed wedding photo to the cover and embellish it
with braided ribbon and a heart locket.

*Recycle your broken pots into lively and beautiful frames and bring a patio gar-
den feel indoors. Make a plaster frame as a base for the mosaic to enhance the
irregular, casual look of terracotta, or revitalize an old frame with this simple
technique. This is a wonderful frame to highlight images of flowers, landscapes,
or other natural images, and it will enhance many decorating schemes, from
European country to American Southwestern.*

terracotta mosaic frame

Makes one frame

1 Follow manufacturer's instructions to mix craft plaster and pour into mold. Allow to
harden; remove from mold. Cure plaster according to manufacturer's recommendations.

2 Use tile nippers to even edges of terracotta pieces if desired. Adhere terracotta to the
front of the frame with tile adhesive or silicone sealant. Let dry completely.

3 According to manufacturer's directions, mix sanded grout with water in a disposable
container until it has a fudge-like consistency. Wearing rubber gloves, spread grout into
spaces between pieces with a grout float or wet sponge, making sure to press grout
firmly into cracks. Follow with another clean, wet sponge to wipe off excess grout. Allow
to dry.

4 Sand rough edges with sandpaper. Clean frame with a damp cloth.

5 Adhere photo corners to the back of the frame to hold a picture or photograph.

VARIATION
*Substitute glass pebbles, broken china or tiles, shells, coins, stained glass, or pebbles for the terra-
cotta pieces.*

MATERIALS
- craft plaster
- picture frame mold
- broken terracotta pot
- tile nippers
- silicone sealant or tile adhesive
- sanded tile grout
- grout float
- photo corners
- general craft supplies

TIPS
*To break terracotta, wrap a pot in several layers of newspaper, enclose in a plastic bag, and tap pot gently with a hammer until
it is broken into pieces of the desired size. Moisten the surface of the terracotta before applying grout so less grout adheres to
mosaic pieces. Spread grout at an angle to the terracotta edges to fill in spaces without forming air pockets. When grout is
partially dry, wipe with a damp sponge to even grout lines and smooth rough edges.*

Carving and glazing a slate frame creates an impressive piece for showcasing a precious photograph. The flower design, provided as a template, accents the natural, outdoorsy feel of the stone frame. Engraving the slate surface requires a high-speed rotary tool and specialized tips, but the result is a unique textured design not easily duplicated by other means. For best results, use acrylic paints that are specially created for painting outdoor concrete and terra cotta.

engraved slate frame

Makes one frame

1 Transfer design from page 287 to the face of the square frame with a water-soluble marking pen. If necessary, enlarge or reduce the template to fit your chosen frame size.

2 Using the rotary tool according to manufacturer's directions, carve the design in the slate frame. Only a light touch is needed; allow the speed of the tool to do the work. Use the silicon carbide tip for large areas of the design, and use diamond point tip to carve tiny detailed areas.

3 Mix one part clear glaze to one part acrylic paint to create color glaze for painting. Fill in the carved design with the colored glazes and paintbrush. Allow to dry.

4 If desired, create a transparent color wash by mixing two parts clear glaze with one part of selected acrylic paint. Apply to entire frame with a small sea sponge; let dry.

5 Apply a finishing coat of clear glaze to front and back surfaces of frame. Let dry thoroughly.

VARIATION
Personalize the frame by engraving names, phrases, or dates. The rotary tool can be used to carve other stone surfaces such as terracotta, quarry tile, and sandstone.

TIPS
Wear safety goggles and a dust mask when using the rotary tool. Use a flexible shaft attachment on your rotary tool for more precise control.

MATERIALS
- square slate frame
- high-speed rotary tool with pointed silicon carbide grinding stone tip and diamond point tip
- water-soluble marking pen
- acrylic paint for outdoor concrete and terra cotta in white, cream, yellow, brown, pink, dark green, light green, and sky blue
- clear glaze for outdoor concrete and terra cotta
- template (see page 287)
- general craft supplies

ARTIST: BRENDA SPITZER

*This beaded mosaic frame is deceptively simple to create by glu-
ing prethreaded beads in rows and removing the thread after the
adhesive has set. Using prethreaded beads saves time, but you
can thread your own selection of beads if desired. The shape of
the beads defines the pattern as much as does the color—experiment with different bead sizes and shapes. The beading glue dries
to a transparent finish, and a final coat is used as a protective
seal for the piece.*

glass-beaded frame

Makes one frame

1 Using medium sandpaper sand the area of the frame to be
beaded. Sketch your desired design on the frame with a pencil.

2 Run a line of glue along the outside edges of the front face of
the frame. Hold a length of threaded seed beads tightly on
both ends and lay into glue. Press beads lightly with your finger
to set into glue, adjusting their position with the edge of a
craft knife if necessary. When glue becomes tacky, carefully pull
the thread through the beads to remove. Repeat for the inside
edge of frame face. Allow glue to dry.

3 Outline the edges of the sketched design with glue. Using the
same technique as in step 2, place a threaded row of mini-bugle
beads along each line, remove the thread when set, and allow
glue to dry.

4 Fill in the interior area of the frame by applying glue to small
sections of the design and applying rows of beads, pushing
threaded rows up against each other with a craft knife, and
removing thread once beads have set. Fill in tight areas with
single beads. When frame is finished, allow it to dry for 24
hours. Apply a light coat of the glue over the entire beaded
surface and dry for one week.

VARIATION

*For festive candle displays, glue rows of beads to glass
votive candleholders.*

TIPS

*Beading the edges of the frame and sketched design first creates a firm guideline for placing the remaining
beads. Allow the "bead guidelines" to dry completely before proceeding with interior bead placement.*

MATERIALS

- finished flatface frame
- tan threaded seed beads
- black threaded mini-bugle beads
- beading glue
- general craft supplies

ARTIST: SANDRA SALAMONY

ARTIST: SANDRA SALAMONY

Whether you're framing three vacation photos, three pictures of children, or three generations of wedding portraits, this solid cherry triptych frame presents them with style. Danish oil brings out the color and detail of the wood grain while protecting its surface, and brass darkening solution applied to bright brass nails creates a weathered appearance that complements the finish of the hinges. The edges of the wood need not be cut perfectly—let the rough-sawn edges of the cherry plank add to the distinctive appearance of this frame.

hinged
triptych frame

Makes one frame

1 Saw the cherry plank into three 6" (15 cm) wide panels and sand edges smooth. Wipe away sawdust with a lightly misted paper towel or a tack cloth. Apply Danish oil with a soft cloth, let penetrate 5 minutes, then wipe off excess according to manufacturer's directions. Repeat after 24 hours. Let dry an additional 24 hours.

2 Lay the three wood panels flat with wood grain matching. Cut a 4" x 6" (10 cm x 15 cm) template from scrap cardboard and mark three edges in 1" (3 cm) increments, omitting one short end for the top opening. Position the template at the center of one panel and mark 17 dots on the wood with a pencil at template marks and corners. Repeat to mark remaining panels. Center hinge over each join, separating the panels enough to clear the hinge pin. Mark and drill starter holes for the hinge screws.

3 Following manufacturer's directions, pour brass darkening solution into a disposable glass jar and submerge the brass pins. When desired tint is achieved, remove the pins from the solution. Rinse immediately with water, and pat dry with a paper towel.

4 Hammer the brass pins partially into the wood panels at each marked dot, leaving enough space between pinhead and wood for glass pane and image. Screw hinges in place, and finish by sliding photos and glass into the "U" created by the nails.

VARIATIONS
Use weathered wood and salvaged hinges for a distressed frame.

MATERIALS

- 7 1/2" x 18" x 3/4" (19 cm x 46 cm x 2 cm) cherry plank
- three 4" x 6" (10 cm x 15 cm) pieces of picture glass
- two 2 1/2" x 2" (6 cm x 5 cm) mission-style hinges
- 51 brass escutcheon pins
- Danish oil
- brass darkening solution
- general craft supplies

TIP

If power tools are not available to cut the cherry plank, have your wood supplier saw the pieces at the time of purchase. If the darkened brass finish of the nail head is partially chipped away when hammering, apply a dab of darkening solution with a cotton swab and wipe away with the water-dampened tip of another swab.

Emily & Spot

BASED ON A PROJECT BY RAYMOND H. STARR JR.

*R*aymond H. Starr Jr. was leafing through some snapshots he had taken of his granddaughter, Emily, when he decided that rather than frame the best pictures, he'd use them in a handmade book. The artist chose seven images that, when arranged in a certain order, told the story of an encounter between a benign-looking but aggressive dog called Spot and a precocious child called Emily. Then he settled on a simple structure for his book: a Japanese stab binding with the boards covered in the same material as Emily's crib sheet. (Getting the material was harder than he expected: It had been discontinued, and he finally had to go straight to the manufacturer for a sheet of it.) The result: a memory book, complete with rubber stamps and photos, that looks at the world through his granddaughter's eyes.

What You Need

Newsprint

Handmade paper

Rubber stamps and ink pads

Book board

Book cloth

Photographs

Paste-paper photo corners

Spray fixative

Acrylic matte medium

Rabbitskin glue

PVA glue

Ruler

step-by-step

1. Making a dummy

Make a dummy for the text block out of newsprint to lay out the pictures and the text. Cut nine pieces of newsprint the size of an unfolded page 6 1/2" x 15" (17 cm x 38 cm), or the size of the available image area. (The actual pages will measure slightly larger, at 6 1/2" x 16 1/2" [17 cm x 42 cm], to allow for the binding.) Then map out the placement of the photos with a cardboard L-shaped template and note the placement of the text and rubber stamps on each page.

2. Making the covers

Cut book board slightly larger than the text block. Each cover will consist of two pieces of book board, one measuring 7 1/2" x 7 3/4" (19 cm x 19.5 cm) and another at 7 1/2" x 3/4" (19 cm x 2 cm). (Use the smaller piece as the spine.) Then cut book cloth into a piece 1/2" (1 cm) larger all around than the overall cover, making its dimensions 8 1/2" x 9 3/4" (22 cm x 24.5 cm). Coat the larger piece of book board with a 50/50 mixture of PVA glue and methyl cellulose, and place it on the book cloth so that there's a small margin of cloth on three sides of the board. Then coat the smaller piece of book board with the glue mixture and place it approximately 1/4" (.5 cm) away from the larger piece of book board to form a hinge. Using a bone folder and additional glue, fold the fabric over the book board, repeating the entire process for the back cover. Decorate the inside of the covers with a paste-paper design.

3. Making the text block

To make lightweight paper more durable, coat it with a layer each of rabbitskin glue, acrylic matte medium, and spray fixative, in that order. Number each page on the spine edge, where it won't be visible when the book is bound, and, using the dummy as a guide, do all the rubber stamping. Finally, mount all of the photos on the appropriate pages using the same PVA-methyl cellulose mixture used on the covers.

4. Binding the book

Because Japanese stab binding does not include a conventional spine, the book will close flat, even with its two-dimensional pages. Or try an alternative binding such as metal posts used for accounting ledgers (available at office-supply stores). To accommodate material pasted onto the pages, simply insert several strips of paper between each page of the book at its spine—they will act as spacers for the pages.

Variation

MS. MANNERS'S GUIDE TO WATERMELON

3 ½" x 5 ½" x ¾" (9 cm x 14 cm x 2 cm)

Here again, Starr has turned snapshots of his granddaughter into a storybook—this time about her unique approach to dining on watermelon.

FUNKY-FOOTED
frame

Add funky polymer clay feet to a foil frame to get an outstandingly unique way to display a favorite photo. An acrylic frame forms the base, making this an easy, fun, and functional project.

MATERIALS	• 9" x 12" (23 cm x 31 cm) red foil • Metallic red polymer clay • 4" x 6" (10 cm x 15 cm) acrylic frame • Double-sided tape or Xyron machine with adhesive-only cartridge • Heavy-duty glue	• Texture sheet • 5" x 7" (13 cm x 18 cm) piece of foam core • Craft knife • Brayer (ink roller) • Scissors

step one

Use a craft knife with a sharp blade to cut a 2½" to 3" (6 cm to 8 cm) opening in the center of the foam core. You can adjust the inside opening to fit your photograph.

step two

Add texture to the foil by embossing a random pattern or by placing the foil over any textured surface (such as heavy lace, wire mesh, carved wood, or images stamped into clay) and running a brayer over the foil or rubbing the foil with your finger wrapped in a soft cloth. You can also texture foil by tapping a pencil eraser or the end of a stylus repeatedly over the entire surface.

step three

Trim the foil to 6" x 7" (15 cm x 18 cm). With the scissors, cut eight 2" x ½" (5 cm x 1.3 cm) pieces of foil from the remaining foil. Apply adhesive to the small foil strips, and press them into or around the outside and inside corners on the foam core frame. Smooth the foil down tightly to the foam core.

step four

Center the foam core frame on the silver side of the 6" x 7" (15 cm x 18 cm) piece of foil. Apply strips of double-sided tape first around the outer edges of the foam core frame and then the inner edges. Remove the paper backing from the tape one side at a time. Then fold the foil up over the edge, and press it down into the tape. Remove the paper backing from tape around the opening. Cut an X shape into the opening, and fold each side around to the back. Using the heavy-duty glue, affix the back of the foil frame to the front of the acrylic frame.

step five

To make the clay "feet," condition the polymer clay, and shape it into a ½" (1.3 cm)-diameter roll. Cut two 2" (5 cm) pieces. Cut each of these pieces in half lengthwise to make four pieces. Taper and shape the end of each piece, referring to the photograph at left as a guide. Bake the clay according to the manufacturer's instructions. Once the clay has cooled, glue the "feet" to the acrylic frame, making sure the frame will stand upright.

variation

You can enhance embossed and textured foils by using paints and markers. Dents in the foil can be filled with paint and details outlined with markers. Add twisted wire hangers or stands of wire to further personalize a frame.

STILETTO
photo holder

Have a blast kicking up your heels with this project. Can you imagine a better use for that "killer" pair of heels sitting in the closet? This project is perfect on a dressing table or bureau to hold snapshots of friends and family.

MATERIALS	
• 3 sheets red foil • Xyron 850 machine fitted with adhesive-only cartridge • Unused high-heeled shoe • Air-dry clay • Scissors	• 18-gauge silver wire • 22-gauge silver wire • Pliers • Glass adhesive • Assorted red and silver beads

1. Apply the adhesive to the wrong side of two sheets of foil using the Xyron machine, following manufacturer's directions.

2. Cover the shoe with the foil. Press some air-dry clay into the inside of the shoe.

3. Bend the 18-gauge silver wire into five spirals of different lengths. Place the remaining sheet of red foil over the shoe opening. Insert the points of the spirals into the clay, and allow the clay to completely dry.

4. String some beads onto the 22-gauge wire. Twist the wire around the shoe, allowing occasional fingers of wire to bend over inside shoe. Glue the wire fingers inside shoe with adhesive, and allow it to dry.

5. Trim any excess foil close to the shoe with the scissors, allowing a few ½" (1.3 cm) tabs to tuck inside the shoe. Glue the tabs inside shoe with adhesive, and let dry.

Artist: Beth Wheeler

Gallery *of Art for Projects*

The copyright-free artwork used in this book can be found on the following pages. It is shown here at full size, according to the actual sizes used in the projects for this book. Photocopy or scan the art to make the projects in this book, and try modifying the sizes and colors to suit a variety of other craft and home decorating applications. When scanning images, set the resolution at 150 (dots per inch), which is ideal for both quality and speed. For more information, see *Modifying Art by Hand and Computer,* on pages 12–15.

LOTUS PILLOW, PAGE 27

INDIAN FOLK ART BAG, PAGE 28

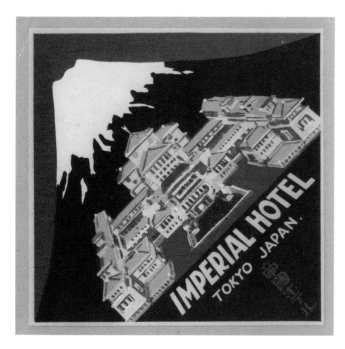

VINTAGE LUGGAGE LABELS, PAGE 31

BUTTERFLY TABLE RUNNER, PAGE 35

WOODEN FRAME WITH BIRDS, PAGE 47

BORDER-FRAMED
MIRROR, PAGE 44

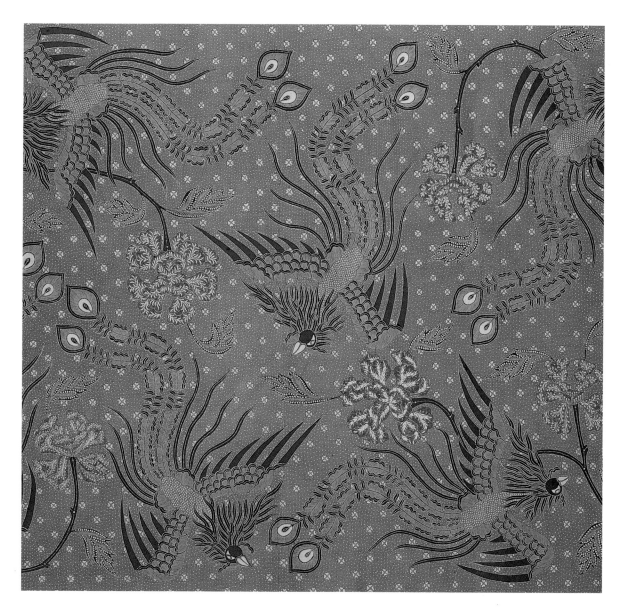

INDONESIAN TABLE RUNNER, PAGE 32

ILLUSTRATED END TABLE, PAGE 48

END TABLE VARIATION, PAGE 51

ENGRAVED SLATE FRAME, PAGE 264

PHOTOCOPY AT 150% OR SIZE TO FIT

FAUX-PAINTED CLOCK, PAGE 52

0 1 2 3 4 5 6 7 8 9

WHITEWASHED CLOCK VARIATION, PAGE 55

STONE TILE COASTERS, PAGE 64

FAUX PORCELAIN PLASTER BOX, PAGE 68

WHITE MARBLE COASTERS, PAGE 67

SQUARE TREASURE BOX, PAGE 71

TERRA-COTTA POTS, PAGE 72

O I 2 3 4
5 6 7 8 9

SALTILLO HOUSE NUMBER PLAQUE, PAGE 76

PENDANT AND PIN SET, PAGE 86

KEYCHAINS, PAGE 89

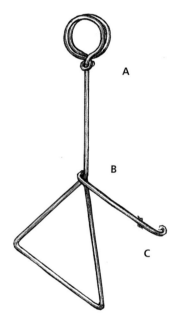

WIRE PHOTO STAND, PAGE 216

TILED BACKSPLASH, PAGE 90

COFFEE BEAN TILES, PAGE 93

MATISSE KITCHEN MAGNETS, PAGE 94

FRUIT AND VEGETABLE MAGNETS, PAGE 97

SUNCATCHER MOBILE, PAGE 98

SILVER-EDGED SUNCATCHERS, PAGE 101

Resources

Aiko's Art Materials Import, Inc.
3347 North Clark Street
Chicago, IL 60657
773-404-5600
fax: 773-404-5919
Japanese paper, bookcloth, tools, books on bookbinding, general art materials

Amaco
American Art Clay Co, Inc.
4717 W. Sixteenth Street
Indianapolis, IN 46222
800-374-1600
www.amaco.com
Metal foil

Amaco (European Office)
P.O. Box 467
Longton, Stoke-on-Trent
ST3 7DN, UK
+01782 399219

API—Crafters Pick
520 Cleveland Avenue
Albany, CA 94710
510-526-7616
www.crafterspick.com

Art Direction Book Co., Inc.
456 Glenbrook Road
Glenbrook, CT 06906
203-353-1441
The Art Direction Book Co. publishes books on graphic design and the *Scan This Book* clip art series.

The Art Store
4004 Hillsboro Pike
Nashville, TN 37215
800-999-4601
www.artstoreplus.com
The Art Store sells supplies for the professional and amateur, including canvases, varnish, and tools.

Art Supply Warehouse
14 Imperial Place
Providence, RI 02906
401-331-4530
Art and journaling materials

Bookmakers International Ltd.
6701B Lafayette Avenue
Riverdale Park, MD 20737
301-927-7787
fax: 301-927-7715
Bookbinding supplies, equipment and tools, books on bookbinding

Cape Cod Cooperage
508-432-0788
Slate frames and plaques

Coomer's Craft Mall
www.coomers.com
Wood shadow boxes, art findings

Crafts a la Cart
P.O. Box 246
Lansdowne, PA 19050
610-394-0992
concraft@aol.com
www.craftsalacart.com
Imported mosaic tiles and related supplies, beads, glad, etching products

D. Brooker & Associates
Rt. 1, Box 12A
Derby, IA 50068
641-533-2103
fax: 641-533-2104
dbrooker@dbrooker.com
www.dbrooker.com
D. Brooker & Associates manufactures several unique wood products, including the ink jet printable wood veneer used in this book.

Dieu Donné Papermill, Inc.
433 Broome Street
New York, NY 10013-2622
212-226-0573
fax: 212-226-6088
Handmade paper, books

Dover Publications
Customer Care Department
31 East 2nd Street
Mineola, NY 11501-3852
fax: 516-742-6953
http://store.doverpublications.com
Dover Publications offers a staggering array of clip art books with themes ranging from cigar box labels to Japanese design motifs. Request a free catalog of clip-art titles by going to the web site or writing to the above address.

Fairfield Processing Corp.
88 Rose Hill Avenue
P.O. Box 1130
Danbury, CT 06813
800-980-8000
www.poly-fil.com
Fairfield sells the Polyfil Extra Loft quilt batting used in the project on page 252.

Fire Mountain Gems
28195 Redwood Highway
Cave Junction, OR 97523-9304
800-423-2319
questions@firemtn.com
www.firemountaingems.com
Fire Mountain Gems sells everything necessary for making jewelry, including semi-precious beads, handmade glass beads, silver and copper beads, wire, findings, and tools.

Iris Nevins Decorative Papers
P.O. Box 429
Johnsonburg, NJ 07846
908-813-8617
fax: 908-813-3431
Marbling supplies, tools, marbling paper; reproduces historical patterns

June Tailor
P.O. Box 208/2861 Highway 175
Richfield, WI 53076
262-644-5288; 800-844-5400
fax: 262-644-5061; 800-246-1573
customerservice@junetailor.com
www.junetailor.com
June Tailor manufactures transfer papers and washable, colorfast printer fabric. Call, write, or email for retailer information.

Pearl Art and Craft
800-221-6845
www.pearlpaint.com
Art, journal, and craft materials

Pearl Paint
308 Canal Street
New York, NY 10013
for domestic mail order, 800-221-6845 x2297;
for international mail order, 212-431-7932 x2297
http://pearlpaint.com
Pearl Paint is a great resource for general art and craft supplies, including metal leaf in several colors, spray adhesive, and tools.

Plaid
P.O. Box 2835
Norcross GA, 30091
800-842-4197
www.plaidonline.com
Plaid manufactures Faster Plaster as well as molds for creating a variety of plaster objects perfect for transfer projects. Visit the Web site or call to order products or to get retailer information.

Polyform Products Co.
1901 Estes Avenue
Elk Grove Village, IL 60007
847-427-0020
www.sculpey.com
Polyform Products manufactures Sculpey brand polymer clay, and Liquid Sculpey, a liquid polymer transfer medium. Visit the web site for tips, free projects, retailer locations, and polymer clay links.

Rag & Bone Bindery

www.ragandbone.com

SoftPen

P.O. Box 1559

Las Cruces, NM 88004

505-523-8820

Photo-coloring pens

TransferMagic.com

P.O. Box 190

Anderson, IN 46015

United States, 800-268-9841; International, 765-642-9308

fax: 765-642-9308

info@transfermagic.com

www.transfermagic.com

TransferMagic.com manufacturers just about everything needed for transferring, including the ink jet *Transfer To Dark* paper used for several projects in this book. They also carry kits and tools for transferring to a variety of surfaces.

Walnut Hollow Farm, Inc.

1409 State Road 23

Dodgeville, WI 53533

800-950-5101

www.walnuthollow.com

Walnut Hollow offers unfinished wood items, including frames, shelves, trays, and boxes. They also sell everything necessary for clock making, which can be purchased separately or in kits.

Directory of Artists

Jane Asper
1357 S. Pennsylvania
Denvor, CO 80210
303-777-3984

Kathy Cano-Murillo
4223 W. Orchid Lane
Phoenix, AZ 85051
623.847.3750
kathymurillo@hotmail.com

Lynne Farris
1101 Juniper Street
Suite 404
Atlanta, GA 30309
404-892-8436

Lori Kay Ludwig
P.O. Box 103
Slippery Rock, PA 16057
724-266-5643
lkludwig@home.com

Barbara Matthiessen
4553 Eastway Drive SE
Port Orchard, WA 98366
360-871-0871
barbaramatthiessen@earthlink.net

Barbara Mauriello
231 Garden Street
Hoboken, NJ 07030
201-420-6613
edmaur@bellatlantic.com

Laura McFadden
49 Vinal Avenue
Somerville, MA 02143
617-625-7906
pluto4@star.net

Livia McRee
62 Church Street, #2F
Wellesley, MA 02482
781-431-0783
livia@liviamcree.com

Sandra Salamony
80 Chestnut Street, #4
Cambridge, MA 02139
617-491-7623
sandranoel@aol.com

Brenda Spitzer
Hand Crafted by Heart
515 South Hale Street
Wheaton, IL 60187
630-682-8405
hcbh@worldnet.att.net

Kelley Taylor
Taylor Design Studio
672 Gateway Drive
Suite 610
Leesburg, VA 02175
703-443-0825

Margaret Tiberio
86 Essex Street, #302
Salem, MA 01970
978-745-4115

Tara Wrobel
P.O. Box 732
West Newbury, MA 01985

About the Authors

Kathy Cano-Murillo is a multi-talented writer and designer. She credits her husband, Patrick, for introducing her to their shared Mexican-American culture. Together they launched Los Mestizos, a business creating Chicano folk art. Her work has been carried in hundreds of shops and museum stores and has been featured in national publications, including *Sunset* magazine, *Gourmet* magazine, and *Latina* magazine.

Lynne Farris is a fabric artist, professional designer, and frequent guest on HGTV and the Discovery Channel. She was trained as a visual artist, began her career as a college art instructor, and then worked for several years in product development in the toy and juvenile products industries. Her work is often published in leading craft magazines, and she works as a creative and marketing consultant to several leading manufacturers.

Mary Ann Hall is a writer and editor with an enduring interest in arts, crafts, and design. She was the founding editor and director of content of Craftopia.com and the editor-in-chief of *Handcraft Illustrated*. As a longtime artist and crafter, she has studied and worked in several areas, including jewelry- and metalworking, painting, polymer-clay sculpture, glassblowing, and furniture making. She lives in Virginia.

Lisa Kerr is a Boston-based author and artist who has been making cards for more than fifteen years. In 1990, her one-time hobby developed in Monolisa Worldwide, a successful business that creates cards, blank journals, and photo albums, and distributes them through gift stores in the U.S. and Europe. Lisa has traveled all over the world, gathering unique papers and techniques to use in her card making. She currently teaches card making in Boston, Massachusetts.

Barbara Matthiessen is a familiar name in the design world. She has authored 37 craft booklets and more than 2,000 magazine articles. She has also contributed her artwork to 12 hardcover craft books. A member of the Society of Craft Designers, she has done product development and consulting for numerous manufacturers, craft retailers, and Web sites. She lives in Port Orchard, Washington.

Barbara Mauriello is an artist and conservator who has a bookbinding studio in Hoboken, New Jersey. She teaches bookbinding and boxmaking at the International Center of Photography, The Center for Book Arts, and Penland School of Crafts.

Livia McRee is a craft writer and designer. Born in Nashville, Tennessee, and raised in New York City by her working artist parents, Livia has always been captivated by and immersed in folk and fine arts, as well as graphic design. She lives in Massachusetts.

Sandra Salamony is an art director and writer living in Cambridge, Massachusetts. She has designed crafts for many magazines and books. She is the author of *Hand Lettering for Crafts*.

Jason Thompson is the founder and president of Rag & Bone Bindery in Providence, Rhode Island, the largest, private hand-bookbinding studio in America solely creating handbound blank books, albums, and journals for the gift and stationery industries. He began journal writing in 1986 while spending a year walking across the country from Los Angeles, California to Washington, D.C. on the Great Peace March, and has been keeping visual journals ever since. He currently resides in Providence, Rhode Island.

Jessica Wrobel's studio work encompasses a range of paper, fiber, floral, and creative package design along with specialties such as handcrafted books, boxes, albums, and fine art papers. Jessica and her husband Tom Eaton are also involved in numerous projects that further arts in their community.